THE BEDFORD SERIES IN HISTORY AND CULTURE

The Rebuilding of Old Commonwealths

and Other Documents of Social Reform in the Progressive Era South

Edited with an Introduction by

William A. Link

University of North Carolina at Greensboro

BEDFORD BOOKS *of* ST. MARTIN'S PRESS

Boston ✄ New York

For Bruce A. Ragsdale, student of the South

For Bedford Books
President and Publisher: Charles H. Christensen
General Manager and Associate Publisher: Joan E. Feinberg
History Editor: Katherine Kurzman
Developmental Editor: Louise D. Townsend
Managing Editor: Elizabeth M. Schaaf
Production Editor: Anne Benaquist
Copyeditor: Nancy Bell Scott
Indexer: Susannah Link
Text Design: Claire Seng-Niemoeller
Cover Design: Richard Emery Design, Inc.
Cover Photograph: Stairway of Treasurer's Residence. Students at Work. Courtesy of Hampton University Archives.

Library of Congress Catalog Card Number: 95–83520
Copyright © 1996 by BEDFORD BOOKS *of* St. Martin's Press

Manufactured in the United States of America.

0 9 8 7 6
f e d c b a

For information, write: St. Martin's Press, Inc., 175 Fifth Avenue, New York, NY 10010
Editorial Offices: Bedford Books *of* St. Martin's Press, 75 Arlington Street, Boston, MA 02116

ISBN: 0–312–10590–8 (paperback)
ISBN: 0–312–12251–9 (hardcover)

Acknowledgments
Pages 106–09: Library of Congress.

Foreword

The Bedford Series in History and Culture is designed so that readers can study the past as historians do.

The historian's first task is finding the evidence. Documents, letters, memoirs, interviews, pictures, movies, novels, or poems can provide facts and clues. Then the historian questions and compares the sources. There is more to do than in a courtroom, for hearsay evidence is welcome, and the historian is usually looking for answers beyond act and motive. Different views of an event may be as important as a single verdict. How a story is told may yield as much information as what it says.

Along the way the historian seeks help from other historians and perhaps from specialists in other disciplines. Finally, it is time to write, to decide on an interpretation and how to arrange the evidence for readers.

Each book in this series contains an important historical document or group of documents, each document a witness from the past and open to interpretation in different ways. The documents are combined with some element of historical narrative — an introduction or a biographical essay, for example — that provides students with an analysis of the primary source material and important background information about the world in which it was produced.

Each book in the series focuses on a specific topic within a specific historical period. Each provides a basis for lively thought and discussion about several aspects of the topic and the historian's role. Each is short enough (and inexpensive enough) to be a reasonable one-week assignment in a college course. Whether as classroom or personal reading, each book in the series provides firsthand experience of the challenge — and fun — of discovering, recreating, and interpreting the past.

Natalie Zemon Davis
Ernest R. May

Preface

Today, many instructors and students approach the topic of Progressivism uneasily. Early-twentieth-century reform seems distant, perhaps even irrelevant; and it is sometimes easy to dismiss as not fitting our contemporary expectations of liberal reform. Still, an understanding of modern America that does not include a full consideration of Progressivism is difficult to imagine. Over the past two centuries, one of the constants of this nation's history has been Americans' interest in altering their social and political institutions to adapt to new circumstances. Progressivism marked a major transition — and an unusual moment — in American history. During the Progressive Era, Americans faced the sweeping economic and social changes that had transformed the country during the previous generation. They responded with reforms of confusing diversity that shared a common objective of expanding the power of public institutions and government in addressing social problems.

Although the literature on Progressivism is abundant, little recent scholarship offers a synthetic, all-encompassing account. Moreover, few primary sources are readily available that display the range of activities and the diversity of settings in which Progressive Era reformers were engaged. This book, exploring some important dimensions of Progressive Era reform, contextualizes them in the distinctive regional locale of the New South. It is concerned primarily with early-twentieth-century social reform and how southerners, white and black, male and female, tried to articulate a vision of a reformed society. That vision, both common and diverse, was united by a consensus among reformers that the South was a poor, economically underprivileged region in need of change and development. But beyond this consensus, sharp differences remained about the future of the New South.

The documents contained in this book follow a format that seeks to present the different dimensions of southern reform. No single document better exemplifies the mood, spirit, and objectives of the Progressive Era in the South than Walter Hines Page's "The Rebuilding of Old Commonwealths." It depicts an underdeveloped region in need of new energy and definitions of individual and community responsibility — a transformation in which education would play a major role. Page's program provides few details about how reform would occur in the New South, although the changes he had in mind clearly went far beyond changing the political system. In the five sections that follow, on race, Prohibition, child labor, black education, and women's rights, divergent reformers present their vision of what Progressive Era reform meant. In reading these documents, students should consider the following questions: What were the goals of reformers and how did they differ? Who would lead the reformed South? What would be the role of government? And how would reforms affect ordinary southerners?

Liberal reformers of the nineteenth and twentieth centuries shared a faith that changes in the law and public policy could successfully alter human behavior. In the South, reformers reinvigorated voluntary groups, churches, and schools; altered the role of government in southern society; and left a lasting legacy of expanded state intervention in areas such as public morality, child welfare, education, and public health. Yet, in practice, the reformers' faith was at least partly naive: The history of reform is littered with examples of reforms that either failed to work or had entirely different consequences from those originally envisioned. Moreover, although working-class, rural, and black Americans sometimes remained indifferent and even opposed to reforms, frequent expressions of cultural, class, and racial superiority accompanied the reformers' faith in the inevitability of their success. Whether or not the results of their reforms lived up to the lofty ideals articulated by Walter Hines Page remains for students of history to judge.

ACKNOWLEDGMENTS

I am grateful for the energetic support of a number of people. When Bedford's history editor, Sabra Scribner, suggested on a bright spring North Carolina day nearly three years ago that I put together a reader on southern Progressivism, she no doubt expected to receive a manuscript sooner than I was able to produce one. Her successor, Niels Aaboe, pushed things along when my pace lagged, and I appreciate his patience as the project took on a different form and as I tried to adapt it accordingly. Charles Christensen helped to conceptualize the book's structure. Like other authors in this series, I benefited from the sage advice and editorial abilities of Louise Townsend, and she skillfully supervised the development of the manuscript from a vague concept to a usable book. I must also acknowledge the help of production manager Elizabeth Schaaf, project editor Anne Benaquist, and copy editor Nancy Bell Scott. Susannah J. Link compiled the index with her usual ability and intelligence.

A number of scholars gave different drafts of the manuscript close scrutiny. Edward L. Ayers, John Milton Cooper, Jr., Charles Eagles, Willard Gatewood, Glenda Gilmore, David Goldfield, Sally McMillen, and Clarence Mohr all read versions, and I am grateful for their knowledge of the sources as well as their advice about the practical realities of using documents in the classroom.

William A. Link

Contents

PART ONE

Introduction:
Social Reform in the
Progressive Era South

In June 1897, a group of young women preparing to graduate from the Normal and Industrial School in Greensboro, North Carolina, heard a startling message from their commencement speaker: Human capital was the South's most important underdeveloped natural resource. Because of an aristocratic and slaveholding past, a rigid social structure, and "worn-out theories," southern people were forgotten men and women — forgotten by both the South's leadership and by their own rapidly changing world. The future was less gloomy: The South, by its own devices, could direct its reinvigoration through intelligent leadership. The key was children, rich and poor. The forgotten men and women would elevate the forgotten child; together, they would construct the foundation of a new social order. With proper direction, even a supposedly "dull" child could someday become "the most capable child in the State." In future generations, a new "patriotic spirit that is our inheritance" would "lift dead men's hands from our stagnant life," a stagnation "baffled by a century's inertia."[1]

The person delivering this bracing message, Walter Hines Page, was a well-known journalist, publisher, and reformer. His ideas about the "forgotten" southern people were not new. In 1881, seventeen years

---

[1] Walter Hines Page, "The Forgotten Man," in *The Rebuilding of Old Commonwealths* (New York: Doubleday, Page, and Company, 1902), 34–35, 46–47.

earlier, as an obscure twenty-six-year-old journalist, he had described "two distinct civilizations," traditional and modern, that existed "plainly side by side" in the South. Although the Civil War had destroyed African American slavery, the Old South survived; southerners still cherished values of gentility, leisure, and idleness. A thriving new society — which many observers were proclaiming a "New South" — was meanwhile emerging, however, and it exhibited hopeful new values of thrift, hard work, and business activity.

According to the young Page, the plantation-based, rural Old South was exemplified in the antebellum (pre–Civil War) gentleman, a former slaveholder of great authority in his community whose use of time was "useless, except in his own estimation." The antebellum gentleman was a talker, and there were "no other men who talk so much, no other men who love to talk so well, and in many instances few men who are able to talk so well." A person of strong opinions, the antebellum gentleman maintained the "very same opinions that he formed years ago"; despite what others outside his world might think, he remained "not a whit less confident of the truth of his own convictions." In contrast, in the same southern community were the merchants, developers, and entrepreneurs — the new men of the South. These men, who exuded a "fresher tone of voice, a more energetic step, a readier wit for a bargain," favored an end to the "immovable prejudice" of antebellum leaders. The division between Old South and New South lay "in the very heart of the people, and comes to view only after a study of their history and their social life." Rejecting many vestiges of Old South civilization, Page preferred a New South that preserved traditions of hospitality and gentility but was forward looking and modernizing in flavor. In a "proper fusion of the old and the new," Page said, the South would realize "a chance for greatness that is almost unparalleled in history."[2]

Page lived most of his adult life outside of the South — he left North Carolina in 1885 — and he achieved recognition as an editor and publisher in Boston and New York. But Page never abandoned an interest in his native region, and, over the next three decades, his analysis of it remained constant. Particularly during the Progressive Era, Page's ideas offer a prominent example, for the American South, of what social reform would mean for one region. For Page, reform necessitated a fundamental change in the direction of the South. Rather than an agriculturally based society, Page preferred an urban industrial world that was closely con-

[2]John Milton Cooper, Jr., *Walter Hines Page: The Southerner as American, 1855–1918* (Chapel Hill: University of North Carolina Press, 1977), 54–55; Page, "Study of an Old Borough," *Atlantic Monthly* XLVII, May 1881, 648–58.

nected to a global economy. He wanted a poor region — at least by comparison with the rest of the United States — to discover a way to develop and modernize. The path toward this social transformation, he concluded, lay in the abandonment of long-held traditions. In all, Page's version of reform — and the version of reformers expressed by many of his contemporaries — was directed to the unique social conditions then existing in the South.

ROOTS OF PROGRESSIVISM

The reform ideas of Walter Hines Page reflected national patterns, for in the decades prior to World War I, a diverse reform movement known as Progressivism affected every region of the United States. Progressives transformed local government, inaugurated statewide nominating primaries, obtained the direct election of U.S. senators, and introduced new powers of government, both state and federal, to regulate business behavior in the marketplace. Significant social reforms accompanied these and other political changes, as state legislatures and the U.S. Congress enacted statewide prohibitions of the sale and distribution of alcoholic beverages, restricted the ability of children to work in industry, established and expanded the role of state government in public schooling and public health, and enfranchised women. Progressivism shared many characteristics. Most reformers came from towns and cities, and they saw public issues from an urban and largely middle-class perspective. Progressives tended to be Protestant, and many joined reform movements because of a new call among many Protestants for Christians to improve their surroundings. And a significant portion of reformers, especially social reformers, were women, many of them middle-class urban women who were beginning to move more aggressively outside of the traditional domestic gender roles of the Victorian era.

The roots of Progressivism lie in the sweeping economic changes occurring during the nineteenth century, when American capitalists constructed a far-flung national transportation network of canals and railroads. The resulting transportation revolution encouraged the integration of local and regional markets into a single, national market economy in which pricing and selling of commodities produced by farms, lumber camps, mines, and factories occurred outside the reach of local communities. The triumph of the market economy, the increasing prominence of railroads as agents and symbols of change, and the emergence of big business — large, national corporations — forced many Americans to reconsider their social, cultural, and political institutions. Their parents and grandparents had inhabited a world that was local and community oriented; their world was increasingly cosmopolitan and driven by impersonal forces. Local government, schools, public welfare, and other social services — whether run by government or private charity — could no longer operate in isolation of developments outside of the community.

As early as the 1870s, a variety of social critics were asserting that American social and political institutions were ill adapted to the new industrial age. In the 1890s and early 1900s, muckrakers, or investigative journalists, published their findings about political corruption and social injustice in glitzy new magazines, such as *McClure's, Cosmopolitan,* and *Munsey's,* that were aimed directly at an urban, middle-class audience. Social scientists such as the economist Richard T. Ely, the sociologist Lester Frank Ward, and the philosopher John Dewey argued that social problems were not an inevitable part of human evolution and that rational, informed leaders might employ purposeful governmental intervention to provide for a better, more efficient, and more just society. Articulating a new creed of liberal activism, the Social Gospel, urban liberal evangelical Protestants such as Washington Gladden and Walter Rauschenbush called for a new social role for Protestants. Rather than an otherworldly paradise, they maintained that the Kingdom of God could be constructed on earth and that it should and could be established through human action.

Further spurring on both criticism and reform of nineteenth-century social, cultural, and political institutions was the mobilization of thousands of women. Although most of them were barred from voting, women increasingly became involved in neighborhood associations, charities, and benevolent societies. Through these local groups, middle-class women exerted influence in areas of home, school, and church. Other women participated in the temperance movement through organizations such as the Woman's Christian Temperance Union (WCTU), which sought to limit and, if possible, eliminate drinking. By the 1890s, large numbers of middle-class urban women were participating in women's clubs, organizations that became involved in local and national public affairs. The emergence of the all-white General Federation of Women's Clubs in 1890 and the National Association of Colored Women in 1895 occurred with significant participation by southern women. Other women became involved in public school reform, early efforts at charity and settlement houses, and urban politics. In big cities, women settlement house workers, such as Jane Addams, who founded Hull House in

Chicago, worked to establish social services for the urban poor — and to advance the definition and response to social problems. Women reformers' call for "municipal housekeeping" was instrumental in shaping public opinion about social and political reform.

Spurred on by Gilded Age critics, reformers captured control of some urban governments during the 1890s. The collapse of public services in Detroit, Michigan, contributed to the election of the reformer Hazen S. Pingree, who was elected on a platform of reform and who served as that city's mayor from 1890 to 1897. In New York, a coalition of reformers were swept into power with the election of William L. Strong as mayor in 1895. Both Pingree and Strong, and many other urban political reformers like them, restructured city government in an effort to make government less partisan, more businesslike, and — to use the buzzword of that era — more "efficient." Elsewhere around the country, political reformers were demonstrating that the traditional operation of elections and government in the nineteenth century had resulted in a pattern of graft, corruption, and poorly administered government.

These attempts to reform local government also affected smaller urban communities. After a hurricane and tidal wave devastated Galveston, Texas, in September 1900 and the government of that city could not cope with the emergency, local leaders banded together to rewrite the local charter. Abolishing the traditional system of government, composed of a board of aldermen, they created a new form of government, with five commissioners elected in an at-large (or citywide) vote. This "commission form" of government quickly became popular around the country, and by 1910 more than one hundred cities — most of them medium sized rather than metropolitan — had adopted it. By 1914, this new form of municipal government had become further refined with the development of the "city manager" plan. It vested all authority in a board of commissioners elected on a nonpartisan basis, and these commissioners were empowered to appoint a city manager, who was expected to be a trained expert in administration and to serve as manager of all departments of municipal government.

PROGRESSIVE REFORM AND ITS CONSEQUENCES

In the first decade of the twentieth century, political reform percolated upward, becoming an important factor in both state and federal politics, and, over the next decade, reformers captured control of state governments from coast to coast. The victory of reformers resulted in significant policy changes. Many legislatures ended the open corruption characterizing mass politics around the nation. New state commissions received the power to intervene in the marketplace. These new commissions limited railroads in their pricing policies (which were widely, if often incorrectly, regarded as exorbitant) and regulated insurance companies. State governments became activist and interventionist in other areas. During the early twentieth century, states restructured public education, not only by expanding public financial support for schools but also by increasing state control through reconstructed school bureaucracies and more effective compulsory attendance laws. Progressive Era state governments established health departments that supervised maternal and child health practices, regulated sanitation and sewage in rural and urban areas, sought to prevent the spread of infectious disease, and attempted to limit longtime scourges such as malaria and venereal disease. State governments also established new standards of child welfare and provided measures for state protection of various forms of labor.

Meanwhile, reformers became influential in national politics as well. The ascent of Theodore Roosevelt to the presidency in 1901 ushered in a new era of presidential activism; Roosevelt, who greatly increased executive powers in both domestic and foreign affairs, embraced the reform cause then emerging at the local and state levels. He favored enlarging the federal government, particularly in its role in the economy. The passage of the Hepburn Act of 1906, followed by other legislation, resulted in new federal regulatory powers over railroads. Theodore Roosevelt was also active in invigorating federal antitrust policies and in transforming federal policies on conservation, natural resources, and land use. During the presidency of Woodrow Wilson, elected to the White House in 1912, federal activism continued, as Congress enacted much of the remaining reform agenda. It established a new, powerful regulatory agency in 1914 in the Federal Trade Commission. Between 1914 and 1916, Congress also created a federally subsidized system of rural credits, a county agricultural extension system, and federal support for vocational agricultural education. It banned the use of child labor on a national basis in 1916, although the Supreme Court subsequently overturned this legislation. And, in the second Wilson administration, Congress enacted both woman suffrage and national Prohibition by constitutional amendment, considered at the time to be crowning achievements of Progressive Era reform at the national level.

It is no exaggeration to say that Progressivism reshaped modern America, and it lies at the heart of the emerging system of government, culture, and society of the twentieth-century United States. While political reform altered the structure of politics, causing major changes in the practice of politics, social reform had an equally significant effect. Prior to the Progressive Era, Americans inhabited a world in which government, especially the federal government, played only a small part. In most areas of life, local government was paramount; nineteenth-century state officials rarely involved themselves in affairs of local communities. Even rarer was the involvement of the federal government, and few Americans felt its direct influence.

Against a backdrop of widespread suspicion toward and inexperience with centralized government, early-twentieth-century reformers advocated major changes. They wanted to expand the reach and effectiveness of government by awarding it the power to regulate areas of life — ranging from private morality to child rearing — that would have been considered out of bounds for eighteenth- and nineteenth-century Americans. Although in implementing these changes reformers confronted a formidable task, they considered government in an entirely new way. Adopting a European model of a rational, professional bureaucracy, early-twentieth-century reformers wanted to re-create government. In place of a passive, nonregulatory government, Progressive Era social reformers favored governmental intervention to regulate business and transportation systems, and, if need be, even control unfair pricing and limit the size of business enterprise. Government, they believed, should have the power to provide for its citizens, even if that meant compelling them to attend school or to follow healthier practices in sanitation. And government, as reformers saw it, should provide for the welfare of its citizens, especially children, even if that meant intervening in the parent-child relationship.

Yet considerable contradication also accompanied these accomplishments. Progressive Era reformers succeeded in transforming the political system, yet through structural reforms such as anticorruption legislation, civil service reforms, and secret-ballot laws, they dealt a blow to the political system — and its highly participatory character. Although women entered the public sphere and were deeply immersed in reform, the extent of political participation — as measured by the number of eligible voters who turned out during elections — steadily declined during the Progressive Era. Political parties, which had formed the bedrock of the nineteenth-century political system, suffered a steady decline from which they would not recover during the twentieth century. The diminishing participation in politics was accompanied by the growing degree to which well-organized, and often well-heeled, groups influenced the political system. At the local, state, and even national levels, interest groups, whose objectives transcended partisan politics, became a new force in politics and governance.

If reform was often undemocratic, it was also frequently coercive. A mass system of education could not be created without greater powers to coerce: School officials had to compel truants and their parents to attend school and to overcome the objections of local communities about the loss of local schools through modernization and consolidation. Public health was impossible unless the public could be persuaded, and often forced, to abandon unhealthy practices of sanitation and health. Children could not be removed from factories unless parents agreed; they usually agreed only when faced with legal sanctions. In short, reform frequently came only through the use of bureaucratic control and state intervention, and reformers were often forced to face the reality that change would not come democratically.

Although Progressivism was a truly national phenomenon, there were important regional distinctions in early-twentieth-century reform. In the North and Midwest, where industrialization and urbanization had made their greatest impact, social reformers concerned themselves primarily with the problems of urban-industrial communities: poor housing, unsafe working conditions, and unacculturated immigrant groups. In the West, reform displayed other characteristics: Among many political reforms, for example, western Progressives sought to create "direct democracy." Through devices such as referenda (in which voters could directly enact laws) and recall (in which voters could remove elected officials before their terms expired) elections, western progressives sought to open up the political system to more direct forms of popular participation. But of all the regional variations of social reform, perhaps the most distinctive appeared in the South, the subject of this collection of documents.

THE MAKING OF THE NEW SOUTH

Like much of the rest of the nation, the South after the Civil War experienced far-reaching economic, social, and environmental changes; unlike the rest of the nation, development and change seemed to accentuate rural poverty and inequality. Well into the twentieth century, a large majority of southerners lived in rural communities. Although the occupation of most of them continued to be farming, the economic status of rural southerners, both white and African American, underwent decline in the post-1865 era. Before the Civil War, farms geared to commercial crops in tobacco, cotton, rice, and sugar depended on slave-labor, plantation agriculture. In contrast, landowning but nonslaveholding southern white farmers — "yeoman" farmers — were able to subsist in large part outside of commercial agriculture; they produced crops such as corn or bred livestock for their own or local consumption.

The Civil War brought major changes. The Thirteenth Amendment emancipated African American slaves, but, without economic skills or resources, freed people constituted a rural underclass. Despite the end of slavery, market-based farming in plantation crops such as cotton actually increased after 1865. The growth of cotton culture was closely connected to the construction, after the Civil War, of a vast railroad network throughout the South. With the further development of a system of agriculture in which prices for crops were determined by national and international markets, self-sufficient, subsistence farms steadily disappeared, and the status of thousands of previously independent yeoman farmers steadily eroded. Both emancipated slaves and impoverished yeomen formed the backbone of a new labor system. Rural whites and blacks alike suffered under a chronically cash-poor economy. Sharecroppers rented their land by promising a future share of their crop to their white landlords; tenants paid landowners a fixed annual rent. Paying high interest charges for the feed and fertilizer that they borrowed from landlords, sharecroppers and tenants found themselves frequently slipping into debt and grinding poverty.

Different changes occurred in the urban South. Although cities such as Charleston, Savannah, and New Orleans flourished in the antebellum South, the post-1865 transportation revolution spurred a new kind of urban community. New towns and small cities dotted the landscape, all of them associated with the new railroad transportation system and the new market economy that accompanied it. The social transformation affecting both rural and urban areas seemed to be remaking the region and creating what some observers were calling a New South that stood in marked contrast to the Old South of plantations and slavery.

In this New South, towns became centers of new forms of enterprise. Some of the new towns grew because of extractive industries in lumbering and mining; others became centers of industrial manufacturing in cotton textiles, tobacco, and iron and steel. Industrial manufacturing — with methods of mass production and factories that revolutionized the industry — helped to spur new boomtowns such as Roanoke, Virginia; Durham, North Carolina; and Birmingham, Alabama. The expansion of cotton textile manufacturing, and the relocation of textile mills from older centers of manufacturing in New England, had an even greater impact across the Piedmont region that stretched from southern Virginia through the Carolinas, Georgia, Alabama, and central Mississippi, as the number of southern cotton textile mills rose from 161 in 1880 to 400 twenty years later.

Three decades of rapid growth in the southern textile industry after 1880 helped to fashion a new industrial working class. Excluding blacks from employment, cotton mills siphoned whites off southern Piedmont and hill country farms; in the two decades after 1880, the numbers of white millworkers thus increased from 16,741 to 97,559. Some of the new mill operatives left farms for factories out of poverty, others because of an uncertain future; most of them lived in mill villages in which the owners provided housing, schools, and churches. In mill villages, workers encountered improved living conditions over what they left behind, but they earned, on average, less than half of the wages of their counterparts in northern mills. Partly because workers adhered to rural patterns of family labor and partly because mill owners wanted a cheap source of workers, a large portion of the southern workforce was composed of women and children. By 1900, three out of ten southern millworkers were children under the age of sixteen; between 1880 and 1900, the number of child workers in textile mills grew 600 percent. Despite working conditions and low wages, the southern industrial proletariat fashioned a distinctive mill culture that was rooted in rural traditions, and it formed a counterpoint to middle classes of New South towns.

The persistence of poverty, despite economic change, became a consistent, if contradictory, theme of the twentieth-century South. Sharecropping and tenancy both increased in the decades prior to World War I; the spread of commercial, plantation crops resulted in increased indebtedness and, in many cases, grinding poverty. Industrialization held great promise for the emergence of a New South; across the region boosters predicted a social transformation that would lift the region out of backwardness. Yet another reality persisted: the lowest wage level in the nation and limited opportunities for millworkers, combined with growing class antagonisms in the mill villages between the urban middle and working classes.

The New South brought racial as well as social stratification. Most white southerners believed that the Fourteenth and Fifteenth amendments, which enfranchised African Americans, were a terrible mistake. Throughout the South, therefore, whites between 1890 and 1906 instituted either constitutional or statutory changes in election law, through such devices as the literacy test and poll taxes, which were designed to bar voting by African Americans. As a result, a significant majority of southern blacks had lost the vote by World War I. Further, southern state legislatures and local governments created a new system of apartheid by enacting legislation requiring rigid racial segregation in public places; these "Jim Crow" laws served as a humiliating symbol of white supremacy. Public resources — care for the infirm and poor, health care, or financial support for public schools — flowed to white and black southerners in a grossly unequal fashion.

THE EMERGENCE OF SOUTHERN PROGRESSIVISM

The dominant leadership of the New South — white, urban, and middle class — saw itself as forward looking and modern, and it endorsed the socioeconomic changes that were affecting its region. By the last years of the nineteenth century, out of the ranks of these men and women came a diverse group of social and political reformers. Although they were enthusiastic New South boosters, these reformers agreed that the South should undergo a thorough modernization. Expressing little nostalgia for old ways, they favored diversified agriculture, the abandonment of reliance on cash crops, and adoption of more scientific farming. They advocated industrialization and for the most part accepted new hierarchies of class and culture that came in the mill village. White reformers also believed that disfranchisement and Jim Crow segregation represented an advance toward stability in race relations.

These men and women supported the same political changes championed by Progressives elsewhere in the United States. They were suspicious of two-party politics, and they favored nonpartisan (without party identification) elections and government. They joined in the rush toward commission and city manager forms of governments. Southern political reformers, like their counterparts elsewhere, embraced a new conception of government, and they enacted new legislation creating state governmental agencies and commissions. Across the South, new state agencies established public control over the activities of insurance and railroad companies in the marketplace. But there was also a distinctive flavor to southern political reform. In state politics, southern reformers merged many of these ideas with a political system that disempowered African Americans; nonpartisan government, to them, meant one-party Democratic government by whites only. The adoption of other reforms such as nomination by political primaries fused Progressive reform with whites-only government.

Meanwhile, southern social reformers turned their attention to the host of social problems afflicting their region. Some of the impetus for reform came from outside the region. During and after the Civil War, northern missionaries became involved in efforts at southern social uplift. Most of these efforts were focused on the education and improvement of emancipated slaves, and northern missionary organizations such as the American Missionary Association established schools and colleges throughout the South during the late nineteenth century. Into the twentieth century, northern missionaries and philanthropists remained committed to African American education, and northerners supported black schools and colleges across the region.

Out of a generation's experience in the South, northern philanthropists significantly expanded their involvement in southern affairs. In 1901, the New York City department store magnate Robert Curtis Ogden, a long-time white supporter and trustee of the all-black Hampton Institute, helped to found the Southern Education Board (SEB); at this organization's creation in Winston-Salem, North Carolina, Ogden transported a large delegation of northerners aboard a private train paid for at his own expense. Out of the SEB, which included both southern white reformers and influential northern philanthropists, grew other efforts at northern involvement. Ogden's efforts attracted the interest of the oil magnate John D. Rockefeller in southern problems — his son, John D. Rockefeller, Jr., attended the Winston-Salem conference — and new Rockefeller philanthropies such as the General Education Board and, later, the International Health Board addressed problems of southern schooling and public health.

Yet strong support and participation in southern social reform originated from within the South. Although there were certainly reformers in the rural South, where more than four-fifths of the southern population then lived, most reformers either lived in New South towns or cities or were closely linked to the new society and economy of the post-Reconstruction era. Unlike the Populists of the late nineteenth century, southern social reformers of the Progressive Era were not interested in restoring a rural commonwealth; rather, they wanted to adapt the South, as quickly as possible, to the ways of the modern world.

The participation and leadership of southern women strongly shaped social reform. In the late nineteenth century, they significantly increased their public activism in local benevolent societies and in women's clubs, and by the early twentieth century they had acquired extensive experience in organizing and participation in public affairs. During the Progressive Era, southern women were directly involved in all of the major social reforms of that time, and a major theme was the convergence of women's mobilization and reform, which culminated in the pre–World War I woman suffrage movement.

SOCIAL PROBLEMS AND SOCIAL REFORM IN THE NEW SOUTH

Social reformers zealously pursued a mission: to alter traditions of southern underdevelopment and backwardness and to modernize the region. For most of them, race was a paramount consideration. Although social reformers agreed that race relations had seriously deteriorated during the late nineteenth and early twentieth centuries, major differences among them remained about the causes and solution of the crisis. Some were paternalists, believing in the need for black progress under benevolent white leadership. Others, in contrast, believed in more radical solutions, such as more rigid forms of segregation.

Most white reformers believed that white supremacy — and disfranchisement and segregation — were necessary preconditions before any political or social reforms could occur. Further, many white reformers believed that there were innate racial differences and that African Americans were racially underdeveloped compared with whites. Despite these racist views, many white reformers exhibited a contradictory approach to African Americans: Although they believed in racial differences and racial hierarchy, in general they also favored the creation of a fair and just society.

Along with race, early-twentieth-century southerners, like many other Americans, saw alcohol abuse and its consequences as the single most critical social problem of their time. During the first third of the nineteenth century, an organized temperance movement had begun around the country. Its main objectives were to limit excessive drinking. Temperance groups such as the American Temperance Society and the Sons of Temperance attracted members committed to partial or complete teetotaling, or abstinence from drinking. The WCTU was actively organizing in the South during the 1880s, but, by the 1890s, the temperance movement had assumed a new character with the rise of the modern Prohibition movement, which was spearheaded by the Anti-Saloon League (ASL). The ASL, which was founded in Ohio in the mid-1890s and first arrived in the South after 1900, focused on a single objective: making saloons and the sale of alcoholic beverages illegal. Drawing on the support of churches, the ASL became one of the most effective interest groups in American history, and during the next decade it succeeded in obtaining local option and statewide Prohibition in many parts of the South.

Most southern reformers agreed that Prohibition was a necessary reform, although they disagreed in their analyses of the best way to accomplish it. Much of the thrust behind Prohibition came from the perception that alcohol abuse, and the male culture of saloons, threatened the family structure and victimized women. In organizations such as the WCTU, established in the 1870s, women had already recognized their central stake in limiting saloons and alcohol abuse. Women continued to play a significant role in the expanded Prohibition movement emerging after 1900. Race also figured prominently. White prohibitionists often cited the race crisis to explain their opposition to saloons. They argued that saloons encouraged a loss of control among whites and blacks; some prohibitionists suggested that eliminating saloons would limit black crime, which they perceived as increasing.

Southern social reformers more readily agreed about children. Since the colonial period, southern (and American) families had seen little distinction between childhood and adulthood; they believed that human personality developed in infancy, without any special needs for protection and parenting. Large families in colonial and nineteenth-century America provided the labor for family farms and workshops, especially the labor of women and children; most children did not attend school regularly. These attitudes changed, however, particularly in urban America. Urban middle-class parents increasingly saw smaller families, child nurture, and schooling as necessary ingredients of proper upbringing; according to this view, childhood was a separate developmental stage. These new attitudes toward childhood collided with rural traditions, for reformers were horrified to discover the extent to which southern white children worked in southern textile mills.

Sporadic efforts occurred throughout the cotton textile South to enact legislation limiting or eliminating child labor in mills. The exposure of child labor helped to arouse southern middle-class opinion. In many southern states, reformers created state anti-child labor committees; in 1904, northern and southern reformers founded the National Child Labor Committee (NCLC). These new conceptions of childhood weighed heavily in educational reform. Nineteenth-century schools in the South, for most children, composed only a part-time experience. Especially in the rural South, children rarely attended beyond the elementary grades; in three or four months of erratic attendance, they acquired little more than literacy and numeracy. Reformers proposed a basic change in the relationship of schools to southern society. They insisted that all children should attend schools regularly and that, if necessary, they should be compelled to attend. Reformers favored modernizing the physical plant of southern schools through the elimination of local, one-room schools and the construction of larger, consolidated schools. They also wanted to enlarge the experience of formal schooling for the southern masses into adolescence by creating high schools. By World War I, school reformers had succeeded in instituting many of these changes throughout the region.

School reform also affected African Americans. Public schools remained symbols of injustice. White schools received increased tax support during the twentieth century, but black schools suffered continued neglect. Despite significant differences about what schooling meant, African Americans and southern white reformers could agree that racial progress depended on education. Northern philanthropy such as the General Education Board and the Anna T. Jeanes Rural School Fund funneled financial support for improved black schools. The Jeanes Fund, which provided for the training of black men and women as Jeanes teachers — who, in turn, supervised the modernization of black rural schools — became one means of African American empowerment. Yet black school reform occurred despite the formidable constraints of rural poverty and halfhearted support from southern whites.

The attempts to transform southern health practices constituted still another important example of reform. Ill health — evident in nutritional deficiencies, rampant and largely untreated disease, and parasitic infection — was a fact of life in the South. After 1865, legislatures established skeletal systems of public health, and state and local officials found an environment of ill health. But perhaps the most important event that exposed the problem of health to southern public opinion, and galvanized Progressive Era public health as a social reform, was the famous hookworm crusade (1909–14). In 1909, Charles W. Stiles, a medical zoologist and discoverer of the hookworm, an intestinal parasite that existed throughout the South because of poor sanitary facilities, persuaded John D. Rockefeller to donate $1 million for the creation of the Rockefeller Sanitary Commission, which led a campaign over the next five years to eradicate hookworm infection in the South.

Although the commission failed in that objective, it did affect attitudes about health. The commission paid the salary of an official attached to the state health bureaucracy; he coordinated a statewide effort to expose and publicize hookworm disease. Commission agents, conducting local campaigns, eventually demonstrated that hookworm was prevalent, infecting perhaps two-fifths of the total southern population. In the most successful campaigns, in North Carolina and Kentucky, Rockefeller officials organized crusades that attracted widespread public interest and support. In other states, however, such as Arkansas, the hookworm campaign was less successful. Nonetheless, when the Rockefeller Sanitary Commission formally disbanded in 1914, it had left an important legacy of structural changes in southern public health practices.

In the Progressive Era South — as in the rest of the country — a distinctive women's political culture accompanied the emergence of social reform movements in temperance and Prohibition, schools, and child welfare. But by World War I many women reformers had concluded that reform, and "municipal housekeeping," depended on the acquisition of political power; some reforming women — although certainly not all — made a connection between reform and the political empowerment of women. Southern suffragists succeeded in mobilizing thousands of southern women: Although not all reformers became suffragists, virtually all suffragists were reformers. Many of them were convinced that the enfranchisement of American women would result in a broader reform triumph.

This connection between reform and political power was immediately apparent to African American women — disfranchised on account of both race and gender — especially those who had become involved in efforts at social uplift. After 1910, most of the South experienced an organized (and in some cases revitalized) woman suffrage movement, as women reformers made a progression from "municipal housekeeping" to campaigns for votes for women. Over the next five years, reformers unsuccessfully attempted to obtain enfranchisement of women by legislative enactment or constitutional amendment. After 1915, the woman suffrage campaign took a new turn, as a majority of southern suffragists worked closely with the National American Woman Suffrage Association (NAWSA) to gain woman suffrage through an amendment to the U.S. Constitution.

Southern social reformers frequently disagreed, as the following documents illustrate, but most of them could agree on the need for a restructuring of southern society from rural, underdeveloped heritage toward a modernized, reformed future. The very nature of reform also raised as many questions as it answered. The most basic of these questions has troubled generations of social reformers, from the nineteenth century into our own time: How could an otherwise apathetic population be convinced of the need for change? The overwhelming majority of reformers, white and African American, were middle class and from towns and cities; the overwhelming majority of southerners were rural and lower class. Not surprisingly, in many instances, reformers and the people that they wanted to reform clashed. Few of the administrative and policy innovations of the early twentieth century occurred without significant opposition, especially in rural communities. Many rural southerners took community control for granted and opposed outside intervention; local communities often rallied against interference by outsiders. Prohibitionists faced the opposition of moonshiners; eventually, widespread opposition and noncooperation doomed Prohibition. Child-labor reformers encountered skepticism from mill owners and resistance from mill parents; both groups resented meddling by outsiders. While school reformers faced significant parental unhappiness with an obvious consequence of reform and modernization — the loss of community control — health reformers frequently encountered community suspicions about compulsory sanitation and outside bureaucratic intervention. Even the woman suffrage movement encountered strong opposition in the powerful antisuffrage movement, which attracted support from around the South.

The efforts of these southern social reformers — and the consequences of their efforts — were diverse and all-encompassing. The following collection of documents exemplifies this diversity. Rather than providing a complete history of reform, the documents focused on representative examples of social reform. The objectives of this collection are to help readers understand the early-twentieth-century South and the character of Progressive Era reform through an array of perspectives. It begins with Walter Hines Page's famous essay "The Rebuilding of Old Commonwealths," in which one southerner analyzed the problems of his native region. The ways in which others defined social reform in the South can be found in the documents that follow. In five sections concerning race, Prohibition, child labor, black education, health, and woman suffrage, the documents of this volume, with section introductions and questions for consideration, illustrate the ways in which black and white, men and women reformers sought social regeneration. As will become obvious, they by no means reached a uniform consensus on these or any issues of the Progressive Era; each section includes sometimes clashing voices, with ample disagreement about the meaning of reform.

PART TWO

The Documents

1

Reforming the New South

Born in Cary, North Carolina, in 1855, Walter Hines Page was a product of the post–Civil War and Reconstruction Era South. Educated at Trinity College (later Duke University), Randolph-Macon College, and the Johns Hopkins University, Page eventually became the editor-publisher of the Raleigh, North Carolina, *State Chronicle*. In February 1885, he left the state and spent the rest of his life in the North, in Boston and New York. In 1887, Page joined the business staff of the *Forum*, in Boston, and four years later acquired control of the periodical; during the 1890s he made it into one of the nation's leading journals of opinion. In 1895, Page joined the staff of the *Atlantic Monthly* and, in three years, became its editor. In 1899, he moved to New York to found a publishing house, Doubleday, Page, and Company, and he was instrumental in acquiring a list of well-known authors such as Theodore Dreiser, Upton Sinclair, Edith Wharton, Woodrow Wilson, and Booker T. Washington.

In New York, Page established a new popular magazine, *The World's Work*, and it became a forum for the investigation of southern social problems. After 1901, Page became a member of both the Southern Education Board and the General Education Board, which included the leadership of white southerners along with northern financial support and which soon became two of the most important organizations advocating reform of southern schools. Later, in 1909, Page also helped to persuade the oil magnate and philanthropist John D. Rockefeller to donate $1 million to establish a commission to examine the public health problem of hookworm infection in the South.

In the following essay, which appeared in the *Atlantic Monthly* in 1902, Page published his ideas for reforming the New South. In reading Page's essay, keep in mind the following questions:

1. What did Page identify as the causes of southern underdevelopment?
2. What elements of the Old South did Page want to change? What elements did he want to retain?

3. How did Page propose to reform the New South?
4. Consider Page's attitudes toward class and race. How did he regard lower-class whites and African Americans in this essay? What role would they play in the "rebuilding of old commonwealths"?

WALTER HINES PAGE

The Rebuilding of Old Commonwealths

1902

I have lately been to a neighbourhood in one of the Southern States that I knew twenty-five years ago. The railway station was then a flimsy shanty that the country merchant had himself built in payment for the railroad's stopping its one daily passenger train if it were signalled. It stopped twice or thrice a week and the passenger who got off or on felt himself a person with privileges. The one daily freight train stopped as seldom; and, when it stopped, it put off a box or a barrel for the merchant, but I think it never took anything on. Three families of importance lived near the railway station, and the little settlement dwindled down the muddy road to a dozen Negro shanties. All round about was a country population on small farms, and further away there were the wrecks of two old plantations.

In the neighbourhood were a Methodist church and a Baptist church. "Mother," said a pious Methodist girl of eighteen, "is it impossible for an Episcopalian to be saved?" For still the circuit-riding preacher at "revival" times insisted that the grace of God fell short of saving them that danced and played cards.[1] The young people and occasionally a hoary sinner went to the mourners' bench and were duly "converted." Then the community rested from disturbing questions of faith till the Baptist "revival" came and the Elder insisted on the necessity of immersion.

There was a shanty down the road that was used for a school-house. A young woman taught a dozen children for $1 a month each till she was married. Then there was no school for two years. For a generation or two

---

[1] Both southern Methodists and Baptists strongly opposed dancing and cardplaying among their members.

Walter Hines Page, "The Rebuilding of Old Commonwealths," *Atlantic Monthly*, May 1902.

it had an intermittent life. A public school was kept for the very poor in a hut a mile away in the woods for about six weeks a year. Life ran easy and life ran slow. Politics and religion, each in its season, the crops and the promise of peaches, stories of fox-hunting and sometimes reminiscences of the war were the staples of conversation.

Two railroads now run by the town and you may take a sleeping car on either one and go to New York in twenty hours, whereas twenty years ago it was a journey of fifty or sixty hours with several stops and there was no sleeping car. The town has mills and shops and paved streets and electric lights, a well-maintained private school and two public schools, one for whites and one for blacks. Society still divides itself into church-groups, but the violence of religious controversy is abated, especially among the men; for they now discuss the price of certain stocks in New York. Even whist[2] parties are held at the home of a man of Baptist antecedents. The men have a wider range of activities and the women have more clothes. The spread of well-being has been general. The intellectual life has been quickened, although it yet shows some of its structural peculiarities. The people are becoming like village-folk wherever they have been touched but not radically changed by material prosperity. If the well-trained reader of *The Atlantic Monthly*[3] who is looking for a problem were now to go to this town, she would go too late; for time is working its natural results in this American community and twenty years hence it will be (except for the presence of two races) very like hundreds of towns in the Middle West. It is true the people talk slowly and cut off their words; they read the worst newspapers in the world because they are "Democratic";[4] but, if they had better cooks, you would be content to live with them the rest of your life, for they give you good fellowship and they have the inestimable boon of leisure.

These good qualities of fellowship and leisure mark them off from the people of corresponding fortune and social gradation in most other parts of the country. They are not only demonstrative; they really care for one another in most affectionate ways. Helpfulness is not an act of conscience: it is an impulse. Hospitality is not a mere habit: it is a necessity of their natures. It was in a town like this that a plan was made to build a hotel; and, when the leading citizen was asked to subscribe to stock in the hotel-company, he replied with a touch of indignation: "A hotel? What do

---

[2] A card game, normally forbidden among southern Baptists, for four players, somewhat like bridge.

[3] A popular periodical, edited by Page, in which this essay first appeared in May 1902.

[4] That is, officially or unofficially affiliated with the Democratic party, then the only effective political party in the South.

you want with a hotel? Whenever a gentleman comes to town I entertain him; and, if a man comes here who isn't a gentleman, let him go on." If you are a gentleman and go there, any man in the town will stop work for a day (or seem to stop it) to entertain you. His household and his business will seem to move wholly with reference to your comfort and convenience; and every man and woman you meet will be delighted to see you. They will tell you so and show you that they mean it. You will come away with the feeling that, though you had before known hospitable individuals and families, you now know a whole town that had nothing to do but to entertain you.

I can never forget or recall without a thrill of gratitude the distinction that was paid me several years ago when I went on an errand to a Southern city where I was almost a stranger. I had been at the hotel less than an hour when a gentleman whom I had not seen for twenty years called and took me to his home. His beautiful children did their share in entertaining me as if I had gone only to see them. I had a letter of introduction to a feeble old gentleman who lived nearly two miles away. I presented it and he seemed overwhelmed with regret that he could not return my call nor add to my entertainment. During my visit the venerable coloured servant of this fine old man rode to the house of my host every morning at eight o'clock and delivered this speech: "De Col'nel sent me to ax consarnin' Mr. Page's helf. He hopes he slep' well an' feels refreshed dis mawnin', and he 'pesses de hope dat you is all well." God rest his soul! he opposed most ideas that I think sound, but he loved all men and women that are lovely and strong; and he was a radiant gentleman.

If you are determined to find a problem, you may reflect on this — how in the march of industrialism these qualities of fellowship and leisure may be retained in the mass of the people; and how they might be transplanted to corresponding towns in other parts of the Union? It is not a trick, not a mere fashion or a tradition: it is a quality of the blood — a touch of nature that would redeem the unlovely wastes of much more prosperous and better-informed life.

A few months ago I rode for more than a hundred miles along this first railway that ran by the village that I have described, in the company of a man who has gradually amassed a fortune by the good management of a cotton-mill. As we passed a dozen such towns he said that he had always believed in the success of "our people." "They are as capable as any people under the sun and are better neighbours than most," said he. "But I had no idea that I should ever live to see such a degree of financial prosperity as they have already reached." Then after a long talk about the growth of these communities he remarked — "Schools, schools, schools of the right sort — that is what we need."

But in the country about these towns men and women are essentially like the men and women who lived there fifty years ago, or eighty years, or even a hundred. The farmers have more money than their predecessors had, but the general structure of their life is the same — a dull succession of the seasons where agriculture is practised in old-fashioned ways, where weary housewives show resignation rather than contentment, and where ignorance has become satisfied with itself. The country is somewhat more densely populated than it was twenty years ago but the growth of population suggests only a denser stagnation.

These men and women do not feel poor. They have a civilization of their own, of which they are very proud. They have for a hundred years been told to be proud of it. The politicians have told them that they are the best people on earth, that the State they live in is the most important in the Union, that the ideas they stand for are the bulwarks of our liberties. Do they not own land? Are they not independent? What more could men ask? One in five is illiterate. But what matter? Some of the illiterate men are more successful than some others that can read. What does it profit a man, then, to read? There is a self-satisfied personal dignity which these men show that prevents near approach. If you propose to change any law or custom, or are suspected of such a wish, or if you come with a new idea, the burden of proving its value is on you. What they are they regard as the normal state of human society. There was talk in one neighbourhood, I recall, about the possibility that the son of one of the more prosperous of these men might go away to study medicine. "I don't see the use," said the father. "We've got two doctors nigh enough and there ain't no room for a third." The preacher, too, has hardened their self-contentment, especially the self-contentment of the women, by fixing their attention on the life to come, almost to the exclusion of ambition to lift up the life that is.

A country schoolmaster in this region told me last year (truly enough) that the ability to read was not a good test even of a man's intelligence, to say nothing of his character. "Why, do you know," asked he, "how many of the Confederate soldiers were illiterate? And they were the best soldiers that ever went to war."

"Suppose they had all been trained — trained to some useful occupation, some as geologists, some as miners, some as machinists, some as shipwrights, some as gun-makers; the iron in Alabama, the wood and coal near by — would these not have been utilized in war?"

"Utilized? We'd 've whipped the Yankees — shore!"

"What would you think of schools where men should now be trained to occupations — schools here in this neighbourhood, to make ploughs, waggons, furniture — everything?"

"That'd be a mighty good thing; but that ain't education."

There is, of course, a considerable variety of social conditions here as everywhere else in the world. Near one home where both children and grandchildren are illegitimate is the residence of a man who holds his land by direct descent in his family from a colonial grant, and whose sons are successful lawyers and preachers in four States. A good many youth go to the towns and find wider opportunities. From this same neighbourhood a young man went to New York and is a rich merchant there; another went to college by his own exertions and is an electrical engineer in a great manufacturing city; another is a partner in a factory in New England; another is a judge in Oregon. The most ambitious, of course, go away; and the general level of life seems to remain as low as it was generations ago. The number of emigrants from the old Southern States tells the story of the stagnation of life in these rural regions.

Three influences have held the social structure stationary — first, slavery, which pickled all Southern life and left it just as it found it; then the politician and the preacher. One has proclaimed the present as the ideal condition; and, if any doubt this declaration, the other has bidden him be content and make sure of the world to come. Thus gagged and bound this rural society has remained stationary longer than English-speaking people have remained stationary anywhere else in the world. It is a state of life that keeps permanently the qualities of the frontier civilization long after the frontier has receded and been forgotten. The feeling that you bring away with you after a visit to such a community is a feeling that something has intervened to hold these people back from their natural development. They have capacity that far outruns their achievement. They are citizens of an earlier time and of a narrower world who have not come to their own. And this is the cue to their character.

The familiar classification of the Southern people as "gentlemen" and "poor whites" is misleading. The number of the large landed proprietors and of large slave-holders has been greatly exaggerated by tradition. Smaller, too, than is thought is the class that may properly be called "white trash" or "buckra." The great mass of these people came of sturdy English and Scotch-Irish stock and they are very like the country population that settled the other States eighty years or more ago. They are not poorer nor "trashier" than the rural population of New Jersey or Pennsylvania or New York or New England were several generations ago, nor than they are now in some remote regions of these States.

If the rural parts of New York or New Jersey or of Pennsylvania were to-day depopulated and all the machinery of the present civilization were removed, and if to-morrow the population of eighty years ago were to reappear just as it was, this would be a community very like these Southern communities. What an interesting field for sociological experiment such a reappearance of a part of the past would present! Peddlers, missionaries, and reorganizers of social life would overwhelm their "contemporary ancestors." It would be a pleasure to help them forward in a decade as far as their descendants travelled in eighty years, but it would not be an easy task. After many impatient efforts we should learn the wisdom of trying to find out their point of view and of contenting ourselves with seeing them advance in their own way, even if they came slowly and seemed stupid. Teaching one's ancestors is at best a difficult undertaking; for it is not the same task as teaching one's descendants. What a lot of disappointing effort this generation might have saved if it had known this simple truth somewhat sooner!

I have purposely not written of the Negro as a separate part of the population, for in the building up of the commonwealth he will yield to the same kind of training. The Negro, at once the beneficiary and the victim of slavery, yet holds the white man, who was its victim and not its beneficiary, in economic bondage; and he is himself also in economic bondage and in bondage likewise to the white man's race-feeling. Training that brings economic independence sets the strongest and most natural forces of life at play. I long doubted whether a democracy could absorb two different races thus living together and yet apart. But the practical results of right training, both on the white man and on the Negro, have left no room for doubt, I think, in the mind of any far-seeing man who has made a personal study of these results. The doubtful thing is whether within any calculable time they will all receive right training.

Without right training, you have such a problem as men nowhere else in our country have. It will yield little to reason. Argument will not solve it. Time alone will bring slow change. The preacher cannot help; for the races have fallen apart in their religious life. The politicians have only made the race-relations worse. The white man has held the Negro back, the Negro has held the white man back; and dead men have ruled them both. Training to economic independence is the only true emancipation.

Distinctive Southern life is to be found not only in the country but in certain old towns also. A college-town will serve as an example. I know such a community where it seems proper to rest till one die, so quiet is its mild, contented life, so dignified the houses and the trees, and so peaceful the half-neglected gardens. You are aware only of an invitation to repose. When a route for a railroad half a century or more ago was run through a college-town very like this there was great excitement. A railroad? Never! It would jar the dignity of the community and corrupt the morals of youth. It was deflected, therefore; and, after thirty years of jolting in hacks over bad roads, the people had to build a branch railroad. But even then they would not permit a locomotive nearer than a mile. The railroad, therefore, ended in an old field and the same hacks yet have their share of work to do. But the old field is now the site of a cotton-mill.

I recently visited a college-town contemporary with this. The century-old buildings, the elms and the oaks that give acres of shade — trees some of which were planted by great men with proper ceremonies — in such an atmosphere generation after generation of youth has absorbed a little learning and much patriotism. The young men you meet are grave in manner, earnest fellows who have already dedicated themselves to the State; for the State is greater than the Nation.

It was in this academic circle more than a decade ago that I asked a member of the faculty why he attended a particular church, for I knew that he had for many years been an "adherent" of another sect and a believer in none. "I throw beef to the lion," said he. "The sectarian representation in this faculty must be evenly balanced, and by this adjustment I belong to the church that I attend." He unlocked a door in his library and took out a handful of books, Matthew Arnold's "Literature and Dogma," a volume of Renan[5] and two or three others. "These I keep under lock and key."

It was in this college-town that I went to rest last winter. My memory will suffer palsy before I forget the unchanging charm of that academic circle of eighteenth-century life; for it is as it was before anything was that now is in our country. The succession of generations is an incident; the coming of men from other States and other lands — it is they that soon change, not this circle into which they come. Tradition is king here and there is no other. You would wear his livery yourself within an hour after you entered his kingdom; and you feel at home, as you would feel at home if you could visit your ancestors from whom you were reprehensible for straying away into your own generation.

When the play of general conversation had ended one evening the talk settled down to a specific topic, and this was the topic — the lack of freedom of speech in the community. Of course, there was in that

[5] Joseph Ernest Renan (1823–1892), a French philosopher and theologian.

company absolute freedom. We were talking about "radical" opinions, especially on theological subjects and about the race-relation. "I should not dare," said one Professor, "to say in public — in my lecture-room or in print — a single thing that I have said here."

"Why?"

"I should be dismissed."

"Do the men who hold the power of dismissal *all* count your opinions a crime?"

"Why, not one of them. They all agree with me. There is no difference of private opinion. I can discuss anything with them in private. But they could not withstand the public indignation that would be expressed through the press."

"This is the more remarkable," another added with a laugh, "because the editor of the most important newspaper in this quarter of the world holds more 'radical' opinions than any other man I know. But he has to serve the public."

"Who is the public?"

"The Democratic platform, the Daughters of the Confederacy,[6] old General So-and-so, and the Presbyterian creed," said one.

"And the farmers who vote whether they can read or not," added another.

As for the editor of the powerful newspaper, I knew that a year before he had sought an engagement in New York in order "to get out of the realm that is ruled by the dead."

It is in such a circle of the old academic society and in rural regions that you come upon the real Southern problem — that unyielding stability of opinion which gives a feeling of despair, the very antithesis of social growth and of social mobility. "Everything lies here where it fell," said a village philosopher in speaking of this temper. "There are the same rocks in the road that were there before the war."

To illustrate — one morning I went to a school for the Negroes and I heard a very black boy translate and construe a passage of Xenophon.[7] His teacher also was a full-blooded Negro. It happened that I went straight from the school to a club where I encountered a group of gentlemen discussing the limitations of the African mind.

"Teach 'em Greek!" said old Judge So-and-so. "Now a nigger could

---

[6] The United Daughters of the Confederacy (UDC) was dedicated to preserving the memory of the "Lost Cause"—the memory of the Confederacy. By this time, the UDC was also an aggressive advocate of the promotion of history written from an admittedly pro-southern perspective.

[7] Xenophon (born about 430 B.C.), a Greek historian and thinker.

learn the Greek alphabet by rote, but he could never intelligently construe a passage from any Greek writer — impossible!" I told him what I had just heard. "Read it? understood it? was black? a black man teaching him? I beg your pardon, but do you read Greek yourself?"

"Sir," said he at last, "I do not for a moment doubt your word. I know you think the nigger read Greek; but you were deceived. I shouldn't believe it if I saw it with my own eyes and heard it with my own ears."

Such are the baffling facts of a sparse population and of a self-satisfied life that lingers past its day. Do they give reason for despair? Not at all; but they do give reason for patience. The problem is the most important that has been presented in our national life. It is not the education of a few millions of neglected persons; it is not the modernizing of a few picturesque institutions; least of all is it the task of imposing on these people the civilization that has been developed elsewhere (for this would be a fool's errand indeed and in no way desirable if it were possible); but the larger question is this:

Since democracy means constant social growth and social mobility, is Southern life becoming democratic or is it remaining stable, or going back to an essentially aristocratic structure? Are forces inside it asserting themselves that give promise of shaping this life in line with democratic growth? Or are the native forces reactionary? Is democracy there at last to be a failure? Is it equal to the task of assimilating the master race and the freed race?

There are thoughtful men who frankly deny the possibility of such a complete conquest by the democratic idea. I quote one such, a man of learning if not of wisdom, who wrote this memorandum for me under the mistletoe in an old South Carolina mansion last winter:

"The dominant elements of society in the two sections of the country were different from the beginning. Slavery did not make the difference, it only emphasized it. The unconscious aims and ideals of the two peoples diverged. The abolition of slavery was a matter of force. So also was the suppression of secession. But these events did not change the essential character of the people. Superficially they are now one. But forty years are as nothing in the life of a people, nor fifty years nor a hundred. The South is to-day further from a willing acceptance of real democratic ideals than it was twenty years ago. The growth of such organizations as the Daughters of the Confederacy, the increasing celebration of the heroism of the Confederate soldier, the silent unwillingness of white men to tax themselves to educate the Negro, the instinctive denial to the Negro of any real standing in the most important matters of life — these things seem to me to point to a different genius, a different tendency, a different ideal, even a different necessity. How the divergence will work itself out, I do not know; but a century hence the South will be, in the essence of its civilization, further from the North than it now is. No outward forms of government can make two different peoples the same."

Another man of learning if not of wisdom used to say to me in Cambridge, Massachusetts: "The Southerners have always seemed foreigners to me. The Northern and the Southern people are different. I do not think they will ever work out the same ideals."

These opinions (which I have heard in recent years only in South Carolina and in Massachusetts and only in academic circles) strip the question of all side issues and of all temporary aspects. It is true that the same laws may not mean the same thing North and South (as the XIVth amendment to the Federal Constitution does not);[8] and forty years have not essentially changed the Negro's place in the community; and it is true that no exterior or temporary influence counts for much and the hereditary "essence of a civilization" is everything. No man of thought has ever regarded laws enacted at Washington against the consent of the Southern people as a primary force in shaping their life, nor outside aid to education or to anything else as revolutionary if it ran counter to the native "genius"; preaching is of no avail; alms-giving is an estranging force; in a word, if Southern life have not in it the seed and the necessity of a true democratic development, then a democratic order cannot be thrust upon it and it were useless to try.

But, if I understand the great forces of our time, and if I know the history of the people of the Southern commonwealths (which to the obscuring of the whole large matter remains unwritten) my friends from whom I have quoted have made a radical misinterpretation of all the large facts and of all dominant present tendencies. There is no undemocratic trait in the Southern people that is not directly accounted for by slavery and by the results of slavery. The most conspicuous institutional results were the political machines that were built on race differences first by one political party and then by the other, and the ecclesiastical machines that are the direct result of popular ignorance and isolation. The country people that I have described are men of good mettle, men to make free

---

[8] The Fourteenth Amendment to the U.S. Constitution, which was ratified in 1868, made freed slaves (and all other native-born Americans) citizens of the United States. As Page suggests, however, the amendment remained at best only partially enforced; both Native Americans and Asian Americans, for example, acquired only partial citizenship until well into the twentieth century. Moreover, African Americans, in the decades after the ratification of the Fourteenth Amendment, never received the full benefits of citizenship and, by 1900, saw the flagrant violation of the terms of the amendment.

commonwealths of. The very strongest impulse they have is patriotic and democratic. The contrary tendencies are clearly survivals of a deflection of their development. So strongly have I been impressed with the democratic quality of Southern character that I believe, if a democracy existed nowhere in the world, Southern life would now evolve one, perhaps even of a radical type.

These old commonwealths were arrested in their development by slavery and by war and by the double burden of a sparse population and of an ignorant alien race. When the weight of these burdens is considered, the progress made these thirty years in the development of the innate democratic tendency is without parallel in our history. The present backwardness of Southern life in rural communities and in old academic or social circles is but a picturesque reminder of the distance we have travelled. Descriptions of these may entertain us, as the charm of the obsolete appeals to all cultivated minds, but they give no hint except by contrast of the real forces of the period in which we live.

The process that has been going on in the upland South in particular is a process of conscious and natural State-building, constructive at every important step. Reactionary influences have been respectable, but they are spent impulses. There are two great constructive forces. The first is Industry, which has already given the essential power over to a class of men that bring mobility to social life and opportunity to them that can take it. This industrial development would finally work out the inherent democratic tendency of the people if no other force were brought into play. But no man who knows the gentleness and the dignity and the leisure of the old Southern life would like to see these qualities blunted by too rude a growth of sheer industrialism.

The other great force that frankly recognizes the arrested development of the people and is taking hold of the problem of their natural growth is the new impulse in public education. This is native, and it is nothing different from Jefferson's creed and plan.[9] So strong is it that its recent manifestation may fairly be called a new chapter in our national history. In the presence of this revolutionary force, fear of reaction and doubt about the democratic "essence" of Southern civilization falls away. Beside this all other forces except the force of industrial life count for nothing.

Formal education has been going on in the South these thirty years with increasing efficiency in the cities and the large towns and at the

---

[9] Thomas Jefferson was an earnest advocate of a system of public education. In 1778, he proposed an ambitious plan of public elementary, secondary, and higher education, but it was rejected by the Virginia legislature.

colleges. There are communities in which the whole attitude towards modern life has been changed by the influence of the schools. But it is not of town life, nor of higher education, that I now write. I write rather of that new impulse for the right training of the neglected masses that is a larger matter than school-room work or academic or professional training — of the subject as it affects the direction of the whole people's development. From this point of view a dozen or two colleges count for little, however excellent they may be; and life in the cities is, in a sense, of secondary importance, because the cities are few and the wide stretches of rural life are almost immeasurable.

The situation is discouraging enough, Heaven knows. In the ten cis-Mississippian Southern States[10] the proportion of illiterate white voters is as large as it was in 1850; and the public schools in these States now give "five cents' worth of education per child per day for only eighty-seven days a year." This is to say that the total expenditure on the public schools is five cents a school-day per pupil and they are kept open an average of only eighty-seven days a year. But it is precisely because the situation is so bad that it is becoming so hopeful. Schools of this sort are little better than none. The people do not care for them. The stolidity of ignorance can not be overcome by any such perfunctory attack as this. The leaders of the best Southern opinion have come to recognize this truth, and they have begun work in a new way. They have discovered that the schools must do something more than teach the three R's, for a people without diversified occupations and without training do not care for the three R's, nor do the three R's profit them greatly. An idle and unproductive man is no less useless because he can read and write.

It was this fundamental fact that General Armstrong saw when he worked out the system of training towards occupations at Hampton Institute for the Negroes;[11] and it is this fundamental fact that the present leaders of popular education in the Southern States understand. They are training hand and mind together. The experience in every rural community where a school of this kind has been established, is that the people who cared nothing for what they called "education" are so eager for this

[10] By "cis-Mississippian"—from the Latin *cis* or "this"—Page means the eastern side of the Mississippi River.

[11] Samuel Chapman Armstrong, a white missionary educator, founded Hampton Institute after the Civil War and became a leading spokesman on black education and a mentor of the prominent African American leader Booker T. Washington. At Hampton and at Tuskegee Institute (which Washington established in 1881), both men popularized a new model of black schooling—"industrial" education—that stressed the acquisition of economic skills and moral training.

training that they will make any sacrifice to obtain it. Herein is the beginning of a complete change in neglected village and rural life. Here, too, is proof that the people are not "in the essence of their civilization" different from the people of the other parts of the country. The "way out" has been found. The problem that the South now presents has at last become so plain that thoughtful men no longer differ about it. It is no longer obscured by race differences, nor by political differences. It is simply the training of the untrained masses. As slavery and war and an isolated life arrested their development and held them in a fixed social condition, so the proper training of them to helpful occupations will release them to usefulness in a democracy.

The new movement is revolutionary for another reason. The old notion of education was that it meant the training of a few. It is now understood that none can be well educated unless all are trained. The failure to educate the masses has sometimes brought tragic results to the educated. There was a man, for instance, in an old Southern town who became a famous scholar in the law; and I suppose that he was a man of very unusual learning. He became a judge, and he was regarded as the foremost jurist in his State. But his income hardly kept his library replenished. He lived in respectable want and died without making provision for his family. His son also was trained to the law; and, since the family felt it a sort of sacred duty that he should remain where he was born, his practice, too, was so small that he became discouraged and his life was a failure. The daughter sold the family mansion to pay the family debts. "But," as one of her neighbours said, "she is the first happy and independent member of that family." She teaches wood-work in the public school, and is training her nephews to scientific agriculture.

The men and women of both races who are leading this great popular movement work with an inspiration that puts conventional teachers to shame. For example: A young agricultural chemist several years ago began with enthusiasm a campaign of education among the farmers. He put much faith in bulletins and leaflets, which were sent broadcast. "I soon found out," said he, "that sending out literature did little good as long as many farmers could not read, and many more would not." He left his laboratory and became an educational statesman, and there are few men in America whose influence in building up the people is greater than his. Out of a comparatively small acquaintance, I know many similar experiences. A well-trained preacher, for example, who has had much to do with the administration of the churches of his sect in rural regions, lately gave up his work and became a superintendent of public schools. "Till the country people are educated," said he, "church work will not stick."

Anyone who knows the work that such men are doing could fill these pages with a bare catalogue of heroic deeds — deeds like these for example: The principal of a school for training white teachers proposed to the faculty that they give a part of their salaries, which were meagre to the edge of poverty, to erect a new building for the school. Not one demurred. The building was put up, but there is yet not room enough for the self-supporting students that apply for admission; and twelve teachers have only four recitation rooms. They are occupied almost every hour of the day. Yet no sooner had their winter vacation come than the principal hurried to Hampton Institute to study its method of teaching handicrafts; and half the faculty went to New York to hear lectures at the Teachers' College.[12] A vacation does not suggest rest to them but opportunity to equip selves better. One of them went, as soon as his vacation began, to organize a model school in a village of two hundred people. They had collected $1,000. He secured $500 from some other source. The building was opened and every white parent in the neighbourhood went to the dedication of it; and the school, with its garden, its kitchen and its workshop as well as its books, provokes such enthusiasm as the community never would have felt for a mere book-school.

Educational work in these States is, therefore, something more than the teaching of youth; it is the building of a new social order. The far-reaching quality of the work that the energetic educators in the South are doing lifts them out of the ranks of mere school-masters and puts them on the level of constructive statesmen. They are the servants of democracy in a sense that no other public servants now are; for they are the re-builders of these old commonwealths.

Any man who has the privilege to contribute even so small a thing as applause to this great movement feels the thrill of this State-building work so strongly that he is not likely to take a keen interest in such tame exercise as historical speculation. Yet it would be interesting to speculate on the effects of Jefferson's plan for public education if it had been carried out. Would the public schools not have prevented the growth of slavery? True, public schools and slavery, as well as most other human institutions, are the results of economic forces; but, if the masses of the Southern population had been educated, or trained to work (and such training is education), a stronger economic impetus might have been given to diversified pursuits than cotton-culture gave to slavery, and the whole

---

[12] Teachers College at Columbia University in New York City had already become a leading national center of pedagogy and education.

course of our history might have been changed. But, whatever may have been the results of Jefferson's educational policy if it had been worked out in Virginia, the development of Southern life in the next hundred years will be determined by the success with which it shall now be worked out. The nature of the problem is clear. The work will be slow and the recovery from these last effects of slavery may require as long a time as it required to abolish slavery; but of the ultimate result no man who can distinguish dominant from incidental forces can have a doubt.

The Southern people were deflected from their natural development. They are the purest American stock we have. They are naturally as capable as any part of our population. They are now slowly but surely working out their own destiny; and that destiny is a democratic order of society which will be an important contribution to the Republic that their ancestors took so large a part in establishing. Rich undeveloped resources of American life lie in these great rural stretches that are yet almost unknown. The foremost patriotic duty of our time is to hasten their development.

2

Race

Although southern social reformers like Page believed that the reinvigoration of the South depended on racial harmony, they also realized that they were functioning in a deteriorating period of black-white relations. The signs of this deterioration were difficult to miss, and many observers described a disturbing breakdown, perhaps even a race war. Lynching became a prevalent form of racial violence and oppression, and it affected black males across the rural South. During the last sixteen years of the nineteenth century, about twenty-five hundred lynchings occurred, an increasing majority of whose victims were African Americans. In the first two years of the twentieth century alone, some 214 blacks were lynched. The urban South saw a similar rise in white-on-black racial violence with the eruption of race riots in Wilmington, North Carolina, in 1898 and Atlanta, Georgia, in 1906. These urban riots, although different in their origins — the Wilmington riot was a politically inspired effort to overthrow a black majority local Republican government, whereas the Atlanta riot was sparked by wild rumors of black assaults of white women — shared the common characteristics of indiscriminate antiblack violence.

A steady decline in the political status of African Americans in the South matched the widespread collapse of racial harmony. The Fourteenth and Fifteenth amendments to the U.S. Constitution provided citizenship to freed people and the vote to freedmen. During and after Reconstruction, southern blacks — despite widespread white hostility and even political terror — not only voted but held numerous political offices. In the decades of the 1880s and 1890s, however, black political rights eroded. The Republican party, which attracted most southern black voters and which provided the chief arena for African American political participation, slowly but surely abandoned the cause of civil rights. Many southern whites saw an opportunity to solidify white supremacy by disfranchising African Americans. Mississippi led the way in 1890 when it provided for a literacy test as a device to exclude blacks during its constitutional convention that year. During the next two decades, other southern states followed suit, disfranchising their African American voters through either literacy tests or poll taxes, which required prepayment of taxes in order to vote.

Disfranchisement effected major changes. In Louisiana, the numbers of registered black voters declined from more than 130,000 prior to disfranchisement to about 1,300 thereafter. In Alabama, heavily black counties saw declines in black registration between 1900 and 1902 from 80,000 to about 1,000 voters. On the heels on this transformation, state legislatures became accountable solely to white constituencies, and they were free to enact new, antiblack legislation. Many of them provided for a new variety of state-required segregation of the races, particularly in railroad, streetcar, and other public transportation. Despite widespread protests by African Americans — including black boycotts of public transportation in a number of southern urban communities — a much more widespread system of de jure (by law) segregation spread across the South. Even more significantly, the expanded system of de jure segregation acquired long-term constitutional status with the U.S. Supreme Court's landmark case *Plessy v. Ferguson* (1896). In this case, the court ruled that laws requiring the separation of blacks and whites in public places — specifically, a Louisiana law segregating the races in public transportation — were constitutional, despite the Fourteenth Amendment's insistence on the equal protection of the laws for all citizens. Laws providing for racial segregation were constitutional, the court held, if they provided "separate but equal" facilities. Although segregation was not new to the South — extensive separation of the races had already existed since the Civil War — *Plessy* permitted, and perhaps even encouraged, a new, antiblack public policy.

It was in this context that white and black reformers confronted the problems of the early-twentieth-century South. Most of them agreed that solving what they called the "race question" — mediating widespread white demands for white supremacy with black demands for racial progress — constituted the major dilemma of their time. Beyond this, reformers diverged significantly, as the documents in this chapter illustrate, about the meaning of the race crisis. African American men and women, as the first two documents suggest, were sorely aware of the symbolic and real humiliations of state-enforced segregation. They suffered daily reminders of white supremacy in public spaces, but they also suffered grossly inequitable distribution of public resources, lack of access to higher-paying jobs, and the absence of legal protections by state and local governments. For African Americans, the "Jim Crow" system of de jure segregation was a daily reality.

Southern whites viewed the race question differently. Reformers, such as Walter Hines Page and Lily Hardy Hammond, concurred that racial harmony was of utmost importance, yet they saw an improvement in race relations as occurring along lines determined by whites. The developments of the 1890s and early 1900s, especially disfranchisement and segregation, seemed to them symptoms rather than the cause of the downward spiral in black-white relations. The real cause, many of them believed, lay in the inadequate "training" that African Americans possessed for freedom. To avoid a general race war, many reformers endorsed disfranchisement and segregation as a "reform" that would ease tensions along lines of indisputed white supremacy. Disfranchisement, many white reformers believed, marked what one of them called a "return of social reason in the South."[1]

Race underlay much of the reformers' view of Progressive reform in the South, but it also raised central contradictions and other issues. When reading the documents in this chapter, consider the following questions:

1. To what extent does each author agree or disagree with Walter Hines Page's view of how best to rebuild the "old commonwealths" of the New South?

2. What perspectives and operating assumptions does each author have? How are these perspectives and assumptions similar? How are they different?

3. How do African Americans such as the anonymous author in the first document and James Dudley in the second document interpret the causes of racial tensions? What suggestions, if any, do they provide for the solution of the race crisis?

4. To what extent does Lily Hardy Hammond, as a white woman, express similar or different attitudes about race, as compared with the African American authors in this chapter?

5. To what extent does Hammond favor racial equality or inequality?

---

[1] John E. White, quoted in Dewey W. Grantham, *Southern Progressivism: The Reconciliation of Progress and Tradition* (Knoxville: University of Tennessee Press, 1983), 117.

The Race Problem — An Autobiography
1904

*Although southerners could generally agree about the worsening environ-
ment of racial relations, they disagreed about its causes. Indeed, there
were sharply different views of how and with what success the segregation
of public spheres of activity in transportation, public parks, and accommo-
dations actually functioned. Most white reformers tended to view both
disfranchisement and segregation as necessary ingredients of reform; although some would admit its failures, the majority of them believed that
both disfranchisement and legally required segregation were ingredients of
racial peace. Clearly, African Americans saw the matter differently. As
the anonymous author of this article believes, segregation was a humiliating symbol of white supremacy and racial oppression.*

My father was slave in name only, his father and master being the
same. He lived on a large plantation and knew many useful things.
The blacksmith shop was the place he liked best, and he was allowed
to go there and make little tools as a child. He became an expert
blacksmith before he was grown. Before the war[1] closed he had married
and was the father of one child. When his father wanted him to remain
on the plantation after the war, he refused because the wages offered
were too small. The old man would not even promise an increase later;
so my father left in a wagon he had made with his own hands, drawn
by a horse he had bought from a passing horse drover with his own
money.

He had in his wagon his wife and baby, some blacksmith tools he had
made from time to time, bedding, their clothing, some food, and twenty
dollars in his pocket. As he drove by the house he got out of the wagon
to bid his father good-by. The old man came down the steps and, pointing
in the direction of the gate, said: "Joseph, when you get on the outside of
that gate — stay." Turning to my mother, he said: "When you get hungry
and need clothes for yourself and the baby, as you are sure to do, come
to me," and he pitched a bag of silver in her lap, which my father
immediately took and placed at his father's feet on the steps and said, "I
am going to feed and clothe them and I can do it on a bare rock." My

[1] That is, the Civil War.

Independent 50 (March 17, 1904): 586–89.

father drove twenty-five miles to the largest town in the State, where he succeeded in renting a small house.

The next day he went out to buy something to eat. On his way home a lady offered him fifty cents for a string of fish for which he had only paid twenty cents. That gave him an idea. Why not buy fish every day and sell them? He had thought to get work at his trade, but here was money to be made and quickly. So from buying a few strings of fish he soon saved enough to buy a wagon load of fish.

My mother was very helpless, never having done anything in her life except needlework. She was unfitted for the hard work, and most of this my father did. He taught my mother to cook, and he would wash and iron himself at night.

Many discouraging things happened to them — often sales were slow and fish would spoil; many would not buy of him because he was colored; another baby was born and died, and my father came very near losing his life for whipping a white man who insulted my mother. He got out of the affair finally, but had to take on a heavy debt, besides giving up all of his hard earned savings.

My father said after the war his ambition was first to educate himself and family, then to own a white house with green blinds, as much like his father's as possible, and to support his family by his own efforts; never to allow his wife and daughters to be thrown in contact with Southern white men in their homes. He succeeded.

The American Missionary Association[2] had opened schools by this time, and my father went to night school and sent his wife and child to school in the day.

By hard work and strict economy two years after he left his father's plantation he gave two hundred dollars for a large plot of ground on a high hill on the outskirts of the town.

Three years later I was born in my father's own home, in his coveted white house with green blinds — his father's house in miniature. Here my father kept a small store, was burned out once and had other trials, but finally he had a large grocery store and feed store attached.

I have never lived in a rented house except for one year since I've been grown. I have never gone to a public school in my life, my parents

[2] The American Missionary Association (AMA) was founded in September 1846 and was composed primarily of northern white antislavery activists. During the Civil War, the AMA deeply involved itself in freedmen's aid activities, primarily the establishment of schools to educate emancipated slaves. Following the war, the AMA survived as the most important national organization supporting black education, and it established numerous black high schools and colleges around the South.

preferring the teaching of the patient "New England schoolmarm" to the Southern "poor white," who thought it little better than a disgrace to teach colored children — so much of a disgrace that she taught her pupils not to speak to her on the streets. My mother and her children never performed any labor outside of my father's and their own homes.

To-day I have the same feeling my parents had. There is no sacrifice I would not make, no hardship I would not undergo rather than allow my daughters to go in service where they would be thrown constantly in contact with Southern white men, for they consider the colored girl their special prey.

It is commonly said that no girl or woman receives a certain kind of insult unless she invites it. That does not apply to a colored girl and woman in the South. The color of her face alone is sufficient invitation to the Southern white man — these same men who profess horror that a white gentleman can entertain a colored one at his table. Out of sight of their own women they are willing and anxious to entertain colored women in various ways. Few colored girls reach the age of sixteen without receiving advances from them — maybe from a young "upstart," and often from a man old enough to be their father, a white haired veteran of sin. Yes, and men high in position whose wives and daughters are leaders of society. I have had a clerk in a store hold my hand as I gave him the money for some purchase and utter some vile request; a shoe man to take liberties, a man in a crowd to place his hands on my person, others to follow me to my very door, a school director to assure me a position if I did his bidding.

It is true these particular men never insulted me but once; but there are others. I might write more along this line and worse things — how a white man of high standing will systematically set out to entrap a colored girl — but my identification would be assured in some quarters. My husband was also educated in an American Missionary Association school (God bless the name!), and after graduating took a course in medicine in another school. He has practiced medicine now for over ten years. By most frugal living and strict economy he saved enough to buy for a home a house of four rooms, which has since been increased to eight. Since our marriage we have bought and paid for two other places, which we rent. My husband's collections average one hundred dollars a month. We have an iron-bound rule that we must save at least fifty dollars a month. Some months we lay by more, but never less. We do not find this very hard to do with the rent from our places, and as I do all of my work except the washing and ironing.

We have three children, two old enough for school. I try to be a good and useful neighbor and friend to those who will allow me. . . .

This is my village, my home, yet am I an outcast. See what an outcast! Not long since I visited a Southern city where the "Jim Crow" car law is enforced. I did not know of this law, and on boarding an electric car took the most convenient seat. The conductor yelled, "What do you mean? Niggers don't sit with white folks down here. You must have come from 'way up yonder. I'm not Roosevelt.[3] We don't sit with niggers, much less eat with them."

I was astonished and said, "I am a stranger and did not know of your law." His answer was: "Well, no back talk now; that's what I'm here for — to tell niggers their places when they don't know them."

Every white man, woman, and child was in a titter of laughter by this time at what they considered the conductor's wit.

These Southern men and women, who pride themselves on their fine sense of feeling, had no feeling for my embarrassment and unmerited insult, and when I asked the conductor to stop the car that I might get off, one woman said in a loud voice, "These niggers get more impudent every day; she doesn't want to sit where she belongs."

No one of them thought that I was embarrassed, wounded, and outraged by the loud, brutal talk of the conductor and the sneering, contemptuous expressions on their own faces. They considered me "impudent" when I only wanted to be alone that I might conquer my emotion. I was nervous and blinded by tears of mortification which will account for my second insult on this same day.

I walked downtown to attend to some business and had to take an elevator in an office building. I stood waiting for the elevator, and when the others, all of whom were white, got in I made a move to go in also, and the boy shut the cage door in my face. I thought the elevator was too crowded and waited; the same thing happened the second time. I would have walked up, but I was going to the fifth story, and my long walk downtown had tired me. The third time the elevator came down the boy pointed to a sign and said, "I guess you can't read; but niggers don't ride in this elevator; we're white folks here, we are. Go to the back and you'll find an elevator for freight and niggers."

[3] The author refers to the famous incident on October 16, 1901, when President Theodore Roosevelt invited the prominent African American leader Booker T. Washington to the White House for dinner. The incident aroused a furor among white southerners, who regarded Washington's visit as violating the southern taboo against socializing, and supposed social equality, between blacks and whites.

The occupants of the elevator also enjoyed themselves at my expense. This second insult in one day seemed more than I could bear. I could transact no business in my frame of mind, so I slowly took the long walk back to the suburbs of the city, where I was stopping.

My feelings were doubly crushed and in my heart, I fear, I rebelled not only against man but God. I have been humiliated and insulted often, but I never get used to it; it is new each time, and stings and hurts more and more.

The very first humiliation I received I remember very distinctly to this day. It was when I was very young. A little girl playmate said to me: "I like to come over to your house to play, we have such good times, and your ma has such good preserves; but don't you tell my ma I eat over here. My ma says you all are nice, clean folks and she'd rather live by you than the white people we moved away from; for you don't borrow things. I know she would whip me if I ate with you, tho, because you are colored, you know."

I was very angry and forgot she was my guest, but told her to go home and bring my ma's sugar home her ma borrowed, and the rice they were always wanting a cup of.

After she had gone home I threw myself upon the ground and cried, for I liked the little girl, and until then I did not know that being "colored" made a difference. I am not sure I knew anything about "colored." I was very young and I know now I had been shielded from all unpleasantness.

My mother found me in tears and I asked her why was I colored, and couldn't little girls eat with me and let their mothers know it.

My mother got the whole story from me, but she couldn't satisfy me with her explanation — or, rather, lack of explanation. The little girl came often to play with me after that and we were little friends again, but we never had any more play dinners. I could not reconcile the fact that she and her people could borrow and eat our rice in their own house and not sit at my table and eat my mother's good, sweet preserves.

The second shock I received was horrible to me at the time. I had not gotten used to real horrible things then. The history of Christian men selling helpless men and women's children to far distant States was unknown to me; a number of men burning another chained to a post an impossibility, the whipping of a grown woman by a strong man unthought of. I was only a child, but I remember to this day what a shock I received. A young colored woman of a lovely disposition and character had just died. She was a teacher in the Sunday school I attended — a self-sacrificing, noble young woman who had been loved by many. Her coffin, room, hall, and even the porch of her house were filled with flowers sent by her friends. There were lovely designs sent by the more prosperous and simple bouquets made by untrained, childish hands. I was on my way with my own last offering of love, when I was met by quite a number of white boys and girls. A girl of about fifteen years said to me, "More flowers for that dead nigger? I never saw such a to-do made over a dead nigger before. Why, there must be thousands of roses alone in that house. I've been standing out here for hours and there has been a continual stream of niggers carrying flowers, and beautiful ones, too, and what makes me madder than anything else, those Yankee teachers carried flowers, too!" I, a little girl, with my heart full of sadness for the death of my friend, could make no answer to these big, heartless boys and girls, who threw stones after me as I ran from them.

When I reached home I could not talk for emotion. My mother was astonished when I found voice to tell her I was not crying because of the death of Miss W., but because I could not do something, anything, to avenge the insult to her dead body. I remember the strongest feeling I had was one of revenge. I wanted even to kill that particular girl or do something to hurt her. I was unhappy for days. I was told that they were heartless, but that I was even worse, and that Miss W. would be the first to condemn me could she speak.

That one encounter made a deep impression on my childish heart; it has been with me throughout the years. I have known real horrors since, but none left a greater impression on me.

My mother used to tell me if I were a good little girl everybody would love me, and if I always used nice manners it would make others show the same to me.

I believed that literally until I entered school, when the many encounters I had with white boys and girls going to and from school made me seriously doubt that goodness and manners were needed in this world. The white children I knew grew meaner as they grew older — more capable of saying things that cut and wound.

I was often told by white children whose parents rented houses: "You think you are white because your folks own their own home; but you ain't, you're a nigger just the same, and my pa says if he had his rights he would own niggers like you and your home, too."

A child's feelings are easily wounded, and day after day I carried a sad heart. To-day I carry a sad heart on account of my children. What is to become of them? The Southern whites dislike more and more the educated colored man. They hate the intelligent colored man who is accumulating something. The respectable, intelligent colored people are "carefully unknown"; their good traits and virtues are never mentioned. On the other hand, the ignorant and vicious are carefully known and all of their traits cried aloud.

In the natural order of things our children will be better educated than we, they will have our accumulations and their own. With the added dislike and hatred of the white man, I shudder to think of the outcome.

In this part of the country, where the Golden Rule is obsolete, the commandment, "Love thy neighbor as thyself" is forgotten; anything is possible.

I dread to see my children grow. I know not their fate. Where the white girl has one temptation, mine will have many. Where the white boy has every opportunity and protection, mine will have few opportunities and no protection. It does not matter how good or wise my children may be, they are colored. When I have said that, all is said. Everything is forgiven in the South but color.

JAMES B. DUDLEY

To Charles Lee Coon

June 4, 1913

This document offers another description by an African American of the daily humiliation of Jim Crow segregation. James B. Dudley (1859–1925), a black North Carolina leader and educator, in 1896 had become president of North Carolina Agricultural and Mechanical College for the Colored Race, which was located in Greensboro. It was founded as a publicly supported college for the state's African Americans, who were barred from entering the all-white public colleges and universities until desegregation during the 1950s. Dudley, like many other middle-class blacks, suffered from the public humiliation of having to ride in segregated railroad cars. In this letter to the white educator and racial moderate Charles L. Coon, he describes his reactions.

My dear Prof. Coon:

I have read your letter of the 2d and I am very much interested in its contents. Your concluding sentence about Negroes, "But no one seems

James B. Dudley to Charles Lee Coon, June 4, 1913, Papers of Charles Lee Coon, Southern Historical Collection, University of North Carolina at Chapel Hill Library, Chapel Hill.

to care" brings to my mind the enclosed Editorial "Who Cares". If you have not read it I shall be glad to have you read, I am sorry to have to trouble you so much, but I would be glad to have it returned.

It is discouraging to us aside from educational matters. I noticed an editorial in the News and Observer[1] a few days ago concerning negroes in Pullman cars calculated to prejudice sentiment against us in protecting our lives.

Every day on the through trains through Greensboro you will see old wooden coaches discarded from the service of white passengers, put immediately behind the engine and immediately in front of steel coaches and heavy Pullman cars for the accommodation of white passengers. These old coaches quite frequently have only one toilet for both sexes, and sandwiched in as they are between the engine and heavy steel cars generally crush like egg shells in case of spreading rails or the train jumping the track, and prove to be death traps for negro passengers. I have frequently read of such cases and just about a year ago a friend of mine who, the only colored passenger with the negro porter, was killed in a wreck while the white passengers enjoying the accommodation of steel coaches were not scratched enough to have to go to the hospital. Now it does seem to me very discouraging that such an influential paper as the News and Observer should use its influence against us in trying to protect our lives by seeking superior protection in the Pullman coaches, especially since in order to avoid these death traps we incur the extra expense of drawing room when a single berth would do just as well.

But amidst all this discouragement we try to be cheerful and believe somebody cares, and that some day the view will be brighter. Our hopes for this brighter day rests largely upon strong heroic men of whom you are a very conspicuous representative.

Very truly yours,
James B. Dudley

---

[1] The *Raleigh News and Observer,* the state's leading Democratic party newspaper, whose editor, Josephus Daniels, frequently engaged in antiblack diatribes.

LILY HARDY HAMMOND

Southern Women and Racial Adjustment

1917

Racial moderation was the rule among southern white reformers. This moderation became particularly apparent among those whites seeking to institutionalize racial cooperation. With the creation of the Commission on Interracial Cooperation in 1919, a new breed of "interracialists" emerged. The interracialists, rather than openly opposing Jim Crow segregation, advocated regular contacts between southern white and black leaders, the support of black institutions, and the amelioration of the worst aspects of segregation. Southern women reformers such as Lily Hardy Hammond (1859–1925) played a significant role in the emergence of interracialism. The daughter of a slaveholder and the wife of the white president of the all-black Paine College, Hammond had supported a variety of social reforms since the 1890s.

The most important source of Hammond's reformism was her involvement with a group of women active in the Methodist Episcopal Church, South. In 1914, Hammond had become first director of the Methodist Women's Bureau of Social Service, and many other southern Methodist women contemporaries figured importantly in the new variety of white racial liberalism. This document illustrates the combination of support for continued segregation and a heightened concern among whites for some variety of racial justice.

The manners and morals of every community reflect the standards sanctioned or permitted by its privileged women. Individuals stand above this common level, blazing ethical trails into the unmoral wilderness of our wider human associations, and draw after them, here and there, adventurous groups; but there can be no mass advance until the individual impulse toward righteousness, which is justice in its finest sense, is reinforced by a common standard embodying a force greater than the individual.

These common standards are furnished, actively or passively, by the privileged women, from whose homes they spread into the community.

Lily Hardy Hammond, *Southern Women and Racial Adjustment* (Charlottesville, Va.: John F. Slater Fund, 1917).

Racial adjustment, like many other moral issues, waits on the leadership of these women. Their attitude toward it is thus of both sectional and national importance; and their increasing development of broad humanitarian standards in racial relations is worthy of note.

New Thoughts for New Times

One great obstacle to better racial adjustment has been the retention by many of us of the viewpoint of a day that is past: our ideal of a good free Negro has been too much like the one that fitted a good slave. Every misfit action has a misfit ideal at its root; and our anomalous crop of racial relations, with its fruitage of lynchings and migrations, is the result of trying to grow the Negro's life to-day on past ideals. Usefulness to his master is a slave's chief virtue; that of a freeman is his usefulness to the human race. However undeveloped or ignorant he may be, the standard of value is shifted at once from an economic to a moral base; and the foundation of all morality is the home. Material progress waits on moral progress; and the full prosperity of Southern industry and commerce waits in a most vital sense upon the moral status of the Negro home. It is the privileged white women who alone can fix this status for the entire community, building it up in white respect, and helping the better class of colored women to build it up in colored life.

The purpose of this pamphlet is to show our women's entrance upon this great humanitarian and patriotic service. To perform it they are adventuring into the unknown, discovering their cooks and washerwomen as women beset by womanhood's clamorous demands and utterly unable to meet them without help and sympathy. It is out of this thought of privileged white women for these handicapped mothers, children, and homes that the eventual adjustment of our bi-racial Southern life will come. . . .

Southern Methodist Women

The first organized body of church women to take up work for colored people was the Southern Methodist Home Mission Society, now merged with the Foreign Society in the Women's Missionary Council of that church. In 1900 they decided to open an industrial department for girls in the school at Augusta, Ga., maintained by their church for the training of colored ministers and teachers. The work met with strong opposition at first, but has won its way to general respect and support, as is evidenced by its increasing development. The Council now operates, in addition to this industrial work, two settlements, one at Augusta, the other at Nashville, Tenn. In both places the Board of Directors is made up of locally prominent men and women of both races. The aim is community betterment, and care is taken to interest the better class of colored people without regard to denominational lines. The older students of the colored normal schools and colleges assist regularly in the club and class work, gaining a measure of training in community work which will bear fruit in their home communities.

The Nashville enterprise has taken on unusual significance, having interested people of both races of all denominations, the Southern white schools, and the colleges for Negroes maintained by Northern people. Courses in Social Service are offered at Fisk University, the field work being done at the settlement under the direction of Southern white women. The National League on Urban Conditions Among Colored People coöperates by maintaining scholarships for these courses at Fisk, which are open to graduates of all colored schools of a certain grade in the South. Vanderbilt University not only furnishes lecturers to these students from its faculty, but students enrolled in the Vanderbilt School of Religion and Philanthropy help in the work of the settlement, thus learning the needs of the colored poor. These initial steps in establishing contact and understanding have already had good results. A Public Welfare League, composed of men and women of both races, is in operation. Its program includes the promotion of a better understanding between the races, the improvement of housing and working conditions for Negroes, and the training of students in methods of community betterment and of race coöperation. This last item is of especial importance, Nashville being to an unusual extent a school center for both races. Among the things already achieved by the Public Welfare League are a public library for Negroes, the organization of probation work for colored juvenile offenders, and two playgrounds for colored children, the city furnishing equipment and salaries, and students trained at Fisk and in the settlement acting as supervisors. A further development of this coöperative spirit was seen after the great fire of 1916, when the white Commercial Club and the Negro Board of Trade worked together in relieving some 1,500 colored fire sufferers.

Local Work of Southern Methodist Women

The undertakings above described are under the immediate care of the women's central missionary organization; but additional work for the 4,700 local auxiliaries has been outlined by the Council. It includes service in colored Sunday schools, promotion of colored missionary societies, school betterment, recreational facilities, and especially the formation of and coöperation with colored women's Community Clubs for betterment along all lines. In the fall of 1915 over 200 auxiliaries were regularly reporting such work. Its effect on public opinion is illustrated by the experience of the superintendent of Social Service for the Louisiana Conference.

"I have changed my views about the Negroes greatly in the last few years," she said recently. "Our Council has educated me; and I think many others feel the same way. A number of our Louisiana societies are working for colored people."

An initial point of contact established, growth in sympathy is certain. Handicapped motherhood and childhood of any race make to privileged women an appeal which is irresistible once it is understood. The women of the North Georgia Conference recently illustrated this fact.

This body has shown by conference action from time to time a broadening sense of obligation to the Negroes; but at the 1917 meeting their growing insight was focused on a wrong which stirs women for women everywhere.

The perennial petition to the next legislature to raise the age of consent[1] from ten to eighteen years was up for its annual endorsement here, as at every gathering of women in the State. This year the W.C.T.U.[2] was leading the fight. In their communication to the Methodist women they referred to the fact that certain legislators had openly objected to the protection the bill would afford colored girls. The W.C.T.U. regarded this an added reason for the bill's passage, and the Methodist women unanimously adopted a resolution calling for "the protection of the childhood and womanhood of Georgia without regard to race." Other bodies of women took the same stand and will keep it until the bill is passed.

Southern Presbyterian Women

These women lead the South in Sunday-school work among Negroes. Some of them have been teaching in colored Sunday schools ever since the war, and of late years the work is spreading. The first wife of President Wilson[3] told the writer that when, as a young girl, she went to New York to study art she sought out a colored Sunday school and taught a class

---

[1] The age of consent was the legal age at which children could engage in sexual intercourse. The legal age of consent before the Progressive Era was, typically, prepubescent.

[2] Woman's Christian Temperance Union.

[3] Ellen Axson Wilson, who died in 1914, was Woodrow Wilson's (president of the United States from 1913 to 1921) first wife.

there the two years she was in the city. She said that if she had come from any section but the South she would have taken some other form of church work; but, being a Southern girl, the daughter and descendant of slave owners, she felt that service to colored people was her especial obligation; and, true to Presbyterian type, she sought a Sunday-school class.

Of late years, however, these women are leading interdenominational organizations of church women in several cities for this and other purposes. The Federation of City Missionary Societies at Meridian, Miss., is typical.

The Presbyterian women led in forming the Federation, which organized an interdenominational Bible Teachers' Training Class from the various colored Sunday schools. It meets weekly in the colored public library with the best white teachers of the city in charge. Then came a Story Tellers' League of the colored teachers. It, too, meets weekly at the library, a white woman telling a story to be repeated by the members at the colored schools. The monthly stereopticon lectures of the Missionary Education Movement are repeated before the colored people; and on one night of Christmas week the Negroes hold a musical service around the municipal Christmas tree.

In Uniontown, Ala., the women of a Presbyterian Bible Class decided to set apart a definite hour each week when each of them would teach the servants in her home the Sunday-school lesson for the next week. This was ten years ago. The basal need in racial adjustment — a human as distinguished from an economic point of contact — being thus met, vision and a broadening service have followed. An interdenominational Bible Class for colored women was formed, officered by colored women and taught by white. Class committees were formed to read the Bible to the colored sick and aged. This brought forward various problems of poverty, and led to relief work guided by the white women and done by the Negro. The children of these homes came into view, and a white teacher maintains for them a weekly story hour.

Institute for Colored Women

A significant development from this widely scattered local work is the inauguration, a year or two ago, of a yearly Institute for Colored Women by the Southern Presbyterian Women's Home Mission Board. It is held at Stillman Institute, Tuscaloosa, Ala., the church training school for colored Presbyterian ministers. In 1916 there were 155 women in attendance from six states. Leading white women were present from the

Board, as well as from Alabama and other states. The courses were given in part by them and in part by colored women. They included Bible study, and lectures on moral training in the home, the home and the school, practical home-making, care of babies, common diseases, sanitation, preservation of food, etc.

A combination of the Methodist Community Clubs conducted by local auxiliaries with a multiplication of such yearly institutes by the general organizations seems an ideal plan for missionary societies to adopt. Both forms of service are closely fitted to the needs of both races; for the rendering of service by those who can give it is as vital to moral health as is the receiving of it by those who need.

Southern Baptist Women

The Baptist Women's Board has no specific enterprise for colored people. They definitely teach, however, through their literature, the duty of local Christian service. This chiefly takes the form of helping the colored Baptist women to form and conduct missionary societies. This practice is widespread. The Home Mission Board has a Department of Personal Service which officially includes work for Negroes; and in several places the coöperation in missionary work above referred to is leading out into the field of social service, especially in those interdenominational missionary federations which are appearing in many of our cities.

A fine instance of local social service was found in Baltimore, where the Baptist women for years carried on a number of industrial schools for colored children. Through the children the mothers were reached, and a strong colored leadership was eventually developed which warranted turning over the work to these women, who have since conducted it.

In Texas a number of auxiliaries are doing work among colored people. In Belton the white college girls, enlisted by the Baptist women, gave a fine missionary program recently in one of the colored churches. In the annual State meetings of the white societies the officers of colored Baptist schools regularly present their work, and a collection is taken for them. In Austin courses in Bible study are given for colored women.

A remarkably successful coöperative work is carried on in Birmingham, Ala., under the leadership of two white missionaries of the Northern Baptist Women's Board. These women have not only a present enrollment of over 700 colored women in their four-year Bible course, but they have enlisted the white women of the city as teachers of these classes. Every denomination is represented, and the teachers have the backing of their local missionary organizations.

Episcopal Women

The work of the women of the Episcopal Church is on a different basis from that of all other churches. It is purely auxiliary to the General Board of Missions, which determines the activities of the women, appropriates the funds raised by them, and is composed entirely of men. This explains their lack of initiative in church work — a lack not found in their Y.W.C.A.[4] or their club work. As church members, however, their directed activities include the work for Negroes maintained by the General Board. This work is larger and better supported by the Southern dioceses than the work for Negroes of any other Southern church, and in this the women have their share. They also share in the local work of the parishes for Negroes, which is chiefly the maintenance of parish schools; and where, as in the diocese of South Georgia, the church employs a trained colored woman for work among her people they give both interest and money to the work. In Tennessee the Bishop has organized a Bishop's Guild among the women for the sole purpose of promoting the educational work of the diocese for Negroes.

The colored women of the dioceses are organized, like the white women, into auxiliaries of the Board of Missions; and the diocesan officers of the white organizations not only attend the annual meetings of the colored women, but assist them throughout the year in their work. In the main, however, the social service activities of these women, as of the women of other denominations, find their largest expression outside of their church organization.

Y.W.C.A. Work Among Colored Women

It seems well to consider this phase of the subject in connection with church work, though it is more recently begun than the club work. For years the only Y.W.C.A. work among Negroes was done from the New York headquarters by a colored secretary in charge of the colored schools. There are now 51 associations in as many schools, and interest is aroused in 50 more. The feeling, however, has been growing among Southern workers that the time has come for coöperative work, and in the fall of 1915 it was decided on at a conference held in Louisville in which women of both races and of both sections took part. A joint committee of Southern white and colored women was formed both to promote the interests of the college associations and to encourage the formation of city associations, independent, and yet linked as "branch associations" to

[4] Young Women's Christian Association.

the central white organization of their respective cities, to which they could look for guidance and coöperation, after the plan found successful in the work for immigrant races in the North. Associations are already in operation in Richmond, Charlotte, and St. Louis, and a number of cities have made application for organization, a necessary feature of the application being the endorsement of the local white association. Jacksonville, Fla., Winston-Salem and Wilmington, N.C., and Lynchburg, Va., are among the cities applying for organization.

Colored student conferences are now held annually in the South, attended by Southern white women. The most promising students are given six weeks' intensive training in the summer at New York headquarters to prepare them for future secretarial work among their people. Conferences are also held on city work, and here both races and both sections are brought together, and a broader basis is being laid for mutual understanding.

Southern Club Women

The facts already recited show Southern women shifting the race problem from a sectional to a human basis, and broadening their adjustment to those Christian standards which fit the whole Race of Man. They are opening the doors of our sectional life to the free winds of world-thought by opening our hearts to the needs of all human life. When one's heart is open to human needs the life of the world flows into it. The smallest, most secluded dwelling place, the daily round of pettiest tasks, is then filled with the throb of a common aspiration, the love of a common justice, the thrill of a universal hope. This liberty of soul our women are achieving for us. Like all the priceless things of life, it lies close to everybody's hand, inextricably tangled in our everyday relations and living. What we need are eyes to see it — a standard of values made visible from the unseen. And this it is the office of women to give.

Their initial inspiration has come from the churches and church teaching, but it is working out, in the main, through organizations outside the church. The beginnings of fifty years ago gathered strength in the W.C.T.U., the first association of women in the South for bettering home conditions. In like manner the social service development of recent years germinated in the church, and there passed its first critical stage; but its flowering is outside the church, as its fullest fruition will be. The church women have created outside of their churches a free, flexible organization to which nothing that concerns human life is alien, and where denominational and class lines do not exist. And here, with the Christian inspiration drawn from their churches, they are, half unconsciously as yet, approaching our old sectional problems from the human, or world, standpoint. The results are already impressive; their implications are greater still. . . .

The Educated Colored Woman

This discovery of the educated colored woman is of deep significance. It is she who must lift her people, but she can do so little without our help! The experience of one club woman is typical here. She seized upon a friend in the street one day to share her recent discovery.

"You know I'm on the committee to meet the colored teachers in the clean-up campaign," she began. " ——— is the chairman of their committee" — naming the head of a local school. "You know she's a college graduate; I've heard about her for years. I thought she'd be a sort of spoiled cook, you know — forward, and all that. Well, she's perfectly *fine*! I didn't know there were any Negroes like that. That committee will work like it was greased. It means everything to the Negroes — and a lot to us, too — to have a woman like that at work among all these colored people here."

Her face was alight with the interest of her discovery — a feeling a number of women are coming to understand as they make similar discoveries in their own communities. Said the president of a city federation in Mississippi lately:

"I had such a sense of adventure when I first began to get acquainted with those women here. You know we couldn't even get the poorer Negroes to clean up except through these educated ones. The first time I went to talk to them about it you can't think how rattled I was. I'd been speaking in public for years, and never thought about being embarrassed. But they looked so different from any Negroes I'd known. I didn't know what their thoughts were like, or how to get at them. I've done some mental gymnastics since, and I trust I'm a broader woman for it."

The outstanding feature of her experience, however, and that of many others, was the finding, in these uncharted regions, the same old landmarks of human need. They are common to all races and all time, and a realization of this fact is one of the things which is helping us to broaden out of a sectional into a world life. . . .

Work of Colored Club Women

. . . What of organized colored women, the other factor necessary to success?

Over 50,000 of them are enrolled in their National Association.[5] They have organizations in thirty states, including all those of the South; and at one of their biennials the writer heard two addresses which for clearness, restrained and forceful speech, and a moral passion rising to heights of genuine eloquence, would have done credit to speakers of any race. The Association publishes a small monthly magazine, edited from Tuskegee by Mrs. Booker T. Washington.[6] It shows these women taking their part in women's world-fight against vice, disease, and injustice; struggling for better health conditions, for home and school improvement, care of children, and all the fundamental interests of women, to whatever race they may belong.

These clubs maintain homes for orphans, old folks, outcast women, working girls; and friendly shelters, day nurseries, and missions. The Teachers' Leagues maintain mothers' clubs, and classes in sewing and domestic science. Work is done for colored hospitals. In Virginia and Missouri the State Associations have secured reform schools for colored girls. In Virginia the organization bought the farm for the school, paying $5,000 cash, and pays about one-third of the yearly expense. The State, with generous assistance from individual white club women, erected the buildings, and pays two-thirds of the running expenses.

The Kentucky State Association has raised in two years $3,000 for improving schoolhouses and helping poor children. South Carolina clubs have in the same time given $1,100 for the same purposes, and over $3,000 for civic and uplift work.

The National Association has a Department of Rural Work, with headquarters at Frankfort, Ky. The chairman has enrolled in her own State, in the last two years, 6,000 women in 670 rural clubs and 362 school leagues. These country women have in that time raised $2,000 for their club work. Yet only 15 of these 670 clubs have joined the national organization.

An Opportunity

This last fact reveals one of the greatest opportunities of our white clubs for a social service to which our whole nation would be indebted — the opportunity to help these struggling, scattered, handicapped women in their efforts to lift the standards of their people's homes.

Few of the colored clubs can afford affiliation with their national or state organizations. Many of them, doubtless, do not yet see the need for

---

[5] National Association of Colored Women, founded in 1895.

[6] Margaret Murray Washington. For further information, see her document "The Gain in the Life of Negro Women," in chapter 6.

wider association; they simply try to minister, in a more or less haphazard fashion, to local needs for which their slender resources are pitifully inadequate. But undoubtedly delegates' expenses and dues to the larger associations are beyond the means of most of them, and so they not only miss the direction and inspiration of contact with their best women, but, missing it, work blindly, their spirit of service often misdirected to ineffectual ends. When their race so suffers for service this waste is genuinely tragic.

For most of these mothers, and the children in their homes, our white women are the only chance for better things. This is also true in the North, where, especially since the exodus, white women have now a chance for this Christian and patriotic service. But we of the South have the right of leadership in this matter, and the signs that it will be exercised are not wanting. The women of Arkansas, of Mississippi, of Baltimore, the women of the various home mission bodies, of the W.C.T.U., and the Y.W.C.A., and of local clubs and societies in every state, are opening doors of service to these isolated, unprivileged women, and guiding them in ways they need to learn. . . .

A Question of Womanhood

The facts herein given, the trend of the movements recorded, tend toward one end: the recognition of womanhood as a thing deeper even than race, a thing for all women to protect. The full recognition of this truth will do more to settle "the race question" than all other things combined, for all other things needed will come out of it — full racial justice, true racial separateness, full human coöperation and respect. The status of the Negro woman and the Negro home in the minds of the privileged white women will determine the status of the race. Among all races, in all times, it has been the lot of the women to bear the unbearable things. As they have won respect and protection the race has climbed toward freedom and self-control. There is no way to raise the Negroes except by this world-old process, and no one can set it in motion as can our Southern white women. . . .

3

Prohibition

When the Anti-Saloon League was first organized in the South in the early 1900s, many observers paid little attention, believing that it was what leading prohibitionist James Cannon, Jr., described as "another spasmodic effort of the temperance cranks, as another wave of enthusiasm, engendered by the appeals of a few fanatical preachers and hysterical women." Even so, the advent of the league was crucial, and it coordinated a mass campaign that swept through the South, gathering momentum as it went. "The breeze became a rushing wind," Cannon wrote, "and the wind became a gale" that burst forth as a hurricane that brought "tireless, persistent, deadly warfare" against saloons and drinking.[1]

In describing the Prohibition movement as a "rushing wind" and "hurricane," Cannon was not exaggerating. Several generations of reformers had attempted to curb the ill effects of alcohol abuse on American society, and since the 1820s various efforts had been made to encourage "temperance," or moderation and, increasingly, abstention, in the use of alcohol. The early temperance reformers were responding to a real social problem: Excessive drinking was widespread in nineteenth-century America, which in the early part of the century was known as the Alcoholic Republic. Although the temperance movement moderated alcohol abuse somewhat, social reformers in the South and elsewhere long identified it as the most important social problem of their time. After the Civil War, many southerners became ardent supporters of temperance; particularly important were the women who participated in the Woman's Christian Temperance Union (WCTU).

But it was particularly during and after the 1880s that a full-scale Prohibition movement emerged in the region. Prior to the advent of the Anti-Saloon League in the early 1900s, prohibitionists in the South remained largely isolated and ineffective. Ohio prohibitionists founded the league in 1895, and its purpose was to mount an aggressive campaign

[1] Quoted in William A. Link, *The Paradox of Southern Progressivism, 1880–1930* (Chapel Hill: University of North Carolina, 1992), 106.

directed, as their name suggested, at the saloon. The tool of the league was state-enforced Prohibition of the sale, manufacture, and distribution of alcohol, but organizers readily adapted their strategy to local and political conditions. Organizing at the grass roots, the Anti-Saloon League orchestrated efforts to ban saloons — and the system by which alcohol was made and distributed — either by local option or by legislative or constitutional amendment.

Prohibitionists promoted an urgent message to southerners, and they firmly identified themselves as part of the effort to achieve a Progressive-style regeneration of the region. Progressive Era prohibitionists were, in fact, less concerned about individual drunkenness than about its systemic cause in the saloon. Reformers identified saloons, and the alcohol abuse that they encouraged, as the cause of myriad social problems: poverty, family breakup, mental illness, and even a wider social breakdown and disorder. Saloons, reformers contended, were centers of crime and prostitution. They filled the jails, reduced the efficiency of workers, and increased the social burdens on everyone. Prohibition, they suggested, would reduce crime and ease social tensions.

At least some white reformers believed that Prohibition would ease racial tensions. Much of the source of racial conflict, according to these reformers, was strong drink, which excited the passions and prejudices of both whites and blacks. The Atlanta race riot of September 1906, in which angry mobs of whites responded to a perceived increase in assaults by black males on white women was rooted in the saloon — at least in the view of many reformers — and in the unleashing of passions among both blacks and whites.

The South proved a fruitful area for prohibitionists in the decades before World War I. A vigorous local option campaign — in which state legislatures permitted counties to institute Prohibition — occurred during the twenty years after 1880, with considerable results. By 1908, to cite three states, 125 of 145 counties in Georgia, 69 of 76 counties in Mississippi, and 94 of 119 counties in Kentucky were "dry" — that is, prohibited the sale of alcoholic beverages. These local option campaigns, under the leadership of the Anti-Saloon League, then blossomed into full-fledged efforts to enact statewide Prohibition. Between 1907 and 1909, in particular, a Prohibition wave struck the South, and six southern states became dry; before 1907, only three states nationally — Maine, Kansas, and North Dakota — had adopted statewide Prohibition.

The documents in this chapter offer some insight into the motives, methods, and objectives of the southern Prohibition movement. Josiah W. Bailey, John E. White, and Booker T. Washington represent a broad

spectrum of opinion and background. Although they would readily agree
with Bailey's characterization of alcohol abuse as the "most serious and
extensive evil of our times in Europe and America," clearly these three
men, and other reformers like them, disagreed about the motives and
method of Prohibition reform in the South.

When reading the documents in this chapter, consider the following
questions:

1. According to the authors, how do their individual visions of
   Prohibition relate to Page's general views on reform?
2. What motives does each reformer express in supporting Prohibition? How do these motives differ?
3. How do the methods of these prohibitionists differ? What justification for their methods do they offer?
4. What effect do the racial attitudes of Bailey and White have on
   their support for Prohibition? To what extent is the perspective
   of Washington, as an African American, different?

JOSIAH WILLIAM BAILEY

The Political Treatment of the Drink Evil

1907

*This document, and the following one by John E. White, illustrate an
important debate among prohibitionists about the methods and means of
accomplishing the end of the saloon. Josiah William Bailey (1873–1946),
who in 1930 was elected to the U.S. Senate from North Carolina, became
editor in 1895 of the* Biblical Recorder, *the Baptist state newspaper in North
Carolina. A leading prohibitionist, Bailey served as head of the state's
Anti-Saloon League from 1903 to 1907. Unlike many prohibitionists, Bailey
opposed Prohibition at the state and national levels, and in 1907 he resigned
his chairmanship of the Anti-Saloon League when that organization became
committed to those methods. Bailey, as he maintains in this article, instead
favored local option as the best method to achieve Prohibition.*

Josiah William Bailey, "The Political Treatment of the Drink Evil," *South Atlantic Quarterly*
6 (Apr. 1907): 109–24.

Extent and Gravity of the Drink Evil

The most serious and extensive evil of our times in Europe and America is the drink evil — indulgence and over-indulgence in liquors that intoxicate. It is likewise the most difficult to treat, having proved so far indeed baffling. Its extent and gravity are universally recognized, but no statesman of the first order, so far as I know, has addressed himself to it; and, I think, for the reason that no satisfying and widely applicable political remedy for it — even for the civic phase of it — has been hit upon. Abraham Lincoln is frequently quoted as having said that "the next snarl" — next after slavery — "we've got to straighten out is the liquor question." But slavery was limited to one section, while the drink-habit is distributed throughout our country. In fact the two evils are in no particular alike. Slavery was superficial; it could be cut off. Drink is a personal habit; it cannot be got at so easily. Slavery could be extirpated by law; the drink evil is to a degree beyond the power of legislation. The sale and manufacture of liquors may be regulated, may even be prohibited; but it is another matter to stay the personal habits of millions.

The most conservative authority, the "Committee of Fifty,"[1] eminent men led by Seth Low, Charles Dudley Warner, Francis G. Peabody, Charles W. Eliot, and Washington Gladden, declared after ten years of investigation that drink is the direct cause of nearly fifty percent of crime and of twenty-five percent of poverty in the United States, and other authorities reasoning from extensive investigations — notably the Massachusetts Bureau of Labor in its 26th Report — attribute to this cause nearly half the cases of insanity. While our annual drink bill, for intoxicating liquors, amounts to one billion five hundred million dollars, a sum that would build several Panama Canals, a tax of more than $20.00 per capita on every inhabitant of the United States, an infusion of injurious intoxicants that not only produces an army of millions of drunkards, whose death-list is 100,000 a year, but impairs the effectiveness of our industrial forces to an incalculable degree — not to mention the vast undermining of moral sense.

Even these most conservative estimates convince one at a glance that here is a field for the greatest service, that here is an evil that demands the wisest and most devoted efforts, that here is opportunity to do a larger good than can be found in any other field, that here is a task and a danger commanding every citizen's attention. . . .

In this article I shall undertake to discuss some of the political efforts to cope with the drink evil, to indicate from American experiments — of

[1] See the report of the Committee of Fifty, published as *The Liquor Problem* (Boston: Houghton Mifflin, 1907).

which there have been many — the only practical and wise political method of dealing with the liquor traffic, and, finally, to set down certain conclusions in general and certain others with special reference to the present North Carolina experiment, of the wisdom of which my study and experience have convinced me. . . .

Our only policy is to maintain our zealous warfare against drink, although, as I propose to indicate, we may more wisely direct our political efforts than we have hitherto. We may protest against misdirected or unintelligent zeal, but we are not wise to protest against the passionate indictments of an evil so ruinous and so extensive. Only let the actual work of drink come home to you, and you will gain an access of sympathy for the intemperate warrior against drink that will quite suffice. A thing so potent to ruin men and destroy homes, an enemy of welfare so persistent, requires and justifies a passionate hatred. But, of course, it is the task of the calmer spirits to wisely direct this passion.

Political Remedies

In response to agitations, many American counties, cities, and states have undertaken to eradicate this evil by political enactments. I think every plan has been tried save national prohibition — high license, low license, no license, substitutes for the saloon, local option, county prohibition, local prohibition, state prohibition, prohibition by popular vote, prohibition by statute, prohibition by constitutional amendment. The Empire of China has recently undertaken the national prohibition of the use of opium, an elaborate plan to extirpate the evil in ten years by imperial decree having been promulgated. It may be possible that such a scheme will succeed in China. But even if it should, we all know that there would be little in the success to encourage Americans. We know that our national power is not sufficient to control in local affairs — constitution or no constitution. To do so would require, not only a China-like centralization, but a China-like power to behead, and, moreover, a practical constabulary occupation of the country. So we may dismiss this delusion of the Prohibition Party, and proceed to discuss the experiments that have been tried.

STATE PROHIBITION

It is of record that state prohibition has been tried in twenty-three states of the American Union. . . .

The conclusion is overwhelming that state prohibition is a failure. North Carolina would be worse off with it than she is without it. She would gain nothing that she now has not; and she would lose the advantage of direct support of local prohibitory measures. I can account, therefore, for the demand in certain quarters for state prohibition only in the general ignorance of its failure wherever it has been tried. And I believe a study of conditions in Kansas and Maine will convince the friends of temperance that we have nothing to gain by following the example of these states.

We may set down as one fact clearly established by experience that general prohibitory laws are ineffectual in cities — as indicated by open saloons in Maine and Kansas.

But there are state laws which are effectual; and we find them in North Carolina. We have in North Carolina state laws prohibiting the manufacture and sale of intoxicating liquors everywhere save in incorporated and policed towns. That these laws have proved reasonably effectual is not to be disputed. But we have no reason to argue that such laws will make good in any other state. They are successful in North Carolina because the population approves them. Many citizens of the rural districts approve them only because they can obtain drink when they go to town. To cut off the town saloons or dispensaries would tend to make these citizens opponents of the present limited prohibitory laws instead of advocates of them. The advocate of state prohibition will be wise to weigh this assertion. For we have proceeded far enough now to say that another fact established by our American experiments in temperance legislation is — *that liquor traffic regulations can be no stronger than the local opinion will bear.*

This is measurably true of any law in a free country. The sovereign is not one, but many. The sovereign is not Congress, is not the General Assembly; the sovereign is the people — and the people are not a nation, nor a state; they are the community — the municipality. Ours is not a government of centralized powers; the power is distributed; and wherever the population is sufficiently organized to govern, there the powers of government in matters pertaining to that locality are deposited; that is to say, if the majority of voters in a city or town or county prefer saloons, they will elect officers that will not molest them, regardless of prohibitory laws. This is done regularly in Kansas, and governor after governor has failed to meet the situation. He may have the mayor indicted; but the people for that very reason re-elect that mayor. To cope with a situation of this kind would require a centralization of authority contrary to all the American precedents and really subversive of the spirit of American institutions. Nothing short of the absolute imperialism of China would suffice — and we shall see whether even that will suffice in China. The theory of self-government is the only theory that civilized people will long tolerate; and self-government does not proceed from the national head downward; it proceeds from the local community upward. . . .

LOCAL OPTION

By local option the regulation of the liquor traffic is referred directly to the electorate upon satisfactory petition — usually one-third of the qualified voters. The voting unit may be the town, the township, or the county. The option may embrace, and, I think, ought to embrace under limitations which I shall tentatively indicate, licensed saloons, dispensaries, and prohibition — these being the three recognized civic treatments of the liquor traffic.

The advantage of local option is that it automatically obtains the support of the majority. The governing power is direct; the voice of the sovereign is obtained. It is of the essence of self-government. Moreover, local option campaigns are educational — they arouse the people, and they place on the people the responsibility which is truly theirs. And since the option is not final, but usually is limited to two years, there is the strongest incentive to the majority to make good their choice. If they establish prohibition, they know that they must make it effectual. If they establish a dispensary, they know that they must see that it is well conducted. If they establish saloons, they know that they must be decently regulated.

It ought to be a fixed rule of American politics never to do for an organized community what it can do for itself; never to accept a responsibility which may be discharged by the electorate. This is self-government. A legislator is foolish to assume the responsibility for an act that his people may conveniently pass upon. His proper duty is to concern himself with the acts of more general import and with only such local acts as are either too insignificant for popular action or that are not worth the cost of an election.

Local option is, therefore, incomparably the best means of treating the liquor traffic.

But there remains the serious question — in local option shall the voting unit be the town, the township, or the county? And there is this other less serious but important question, Shall the option in all cases embrace saloons, dispensaries, and prohibition?

The first question is a question wholly of preponderating interest. For example, Do saloons in Asheville, North Carolina, affect Buncombe county more than they affect Asheville, or so much that Buncombe county voters should have a voice in the option? I would say not. Asheville has a large population — about 17,000. She elects her own officers and is fully competent to govern herself. In fact no one else, either by law or opinion, can govern her. Moreover, her interests in the matter stand above the interests of the county. To permit the county to govern in the matter, say, to thrust prohibition upon Asheville, would be to invite nullification; for it will fall upon Asheville to enforce the prohibition. And I recur here to my statement that the one thing we have learned from our American experiments is that direct opinion and direct control are essential to the success of prohibitory enactments.

But there is in Buncombe county a town named Fairview — a small town. Should that town have the right to set up saloons or dispensaries? Clearly not. The preponderating interest is in the country round about. The vote on a question of this kind should be in the township; and if saloons there would affect a larger territory, that too must be considered. Again, take for example a town of 2,500 inhabitants in a county of 20,000 inhabitants. I take it that here the preponderating interest would be in the county — and would refer the option to the whole county, especially if the town is the county-seat. Otherwise, probably, to the township.

Of course it might be argued that if the law cannot be enforced upon a city of 15,000 population by a county, a county or township cannot enforce the law upon a town of 3,000 population. But I think it will be agreed that ordinarily this will not hold. Opinion would overcome the local disinclination to enforce the law.

Evidently it is necessary to draw a line determining this matter of preponderating interest. It might be done by the ratio of population; it would more wisely be done, if it were practicable, by direct testimony. But in lieu of an example of either of these methods I shall here venture a practical scheme, as follows:

Proclaim prohibition, with no option whatever in all rural districts, including towns of less than 500 population.

Allow option of prohibition or dispensary in towns of more than 500 and less than 3,000 population, giving the county the privilege of ratifying or repudiating the action of the town, if the town is the county seat, provided one-third of the qualified voters of the county (outside the town) petition for the privilege.

With regards to towns that are not county-seats apply the foregoing to the township.

Allow option of prohibition, dispensary, or saloons to towns of more than 3,000 and less than 6,000 population, giving the county, upon petition of one-third of the voters (outside the town) the right to ratify or repudiate the option.

Allow option of prohibition, dispensary, or saloons to cities of 6,000 or more population.

An act of this sort would relieve the General Assembly once and for all of dealing with the liquor traffic — the question would become wholly local, as it should be. It would place the responsibility where it must ultimately rest. It would bring public opinion directly to the support of the law. And, I venture, it would measurably answer the difficult question of preponderating interest.

Experiments in North Carolina

The act of 1903 (Watts act) excluded saloons and distilleries from rural districts in North Carolina. It did not affect many saloons, as for twenty years local laws (acts incorporating churches and school houses with the one object of prohibiting manufacture or sale of liquor within from three to five miles of them) had driven the saloons to the towns. But it did affect 500 distilleries, all but about fifty of which went out of business or became illicit and brought the state and federal officers into the field against them. The act of 1905 further restricted the sale of liquor by confining it not only to incorporated towns, but to incorporated towns that maintained at least two policemen — the principle of the act being that since saloons breed crime they must not exist save where police protection exists. The act went a degree farther with regard to distilleries, forbidding their existence in towns of less than 1,000 population — on the ground that distilleries were likely to be able to dominate and debauch towns of less population.

The act of 1903 also provided local option machinery for all the towns in North Carolina that did not have prohibition or dispensaries by special statute; and this local option offers choice, upon proper petition of one-third of the qualified voters, of prohibition, dispensary, or saloons — the petitioners determining the alternatives.

So we have in North Carolina:

1. Rural prohibition by statute.
2. Municipal local option, under which we have prohibition, dispensaries, and saloons.
3. Statutory prohibition in certain counties and towns. Statutory dispensaries in certain towns. Prohibition in many small towns by special provision in their charters.

It is the overwhelming opinion that this situation is satisfactory. It gives statutory prohibition where prohibition will hold; for the rest it adapts the law to public opinion. The one source of uneasiness is those towns that have special statutes which prevent local option. From them delegations come frequently to the General Assembly, because their only appeal is to that body. The remedy for this is, of course, to give them local option. There are, to be sure, many towns and counties that are content with statutory prohibition, and they resent any proposal of local option for them. This is very well. If they do not want to vote, they should not be invited to do so. But the General Assembly ought to make a rule of giving local option to these towns upon the first manifestation of intention to fight the battle over again in the General Assembly. That is not the place for final settlement of this question.

Rural prohibition has proved entirely satisfactory. Here and there a political demagogue has sought to inflame the minds of the country people with the statement that they are not allowed to vote on liquor questions. But this has had no effect, for good reasons. In the first place the country people have never been in the habit of voting on this question. In the second they are largely opposed to having wayside saloons. If they had a vote they would vote to have what they now have. They enjoy, therefore, their present immunity from those who might involve them in an election on this subject.

Local option elections have gone largely against the saloons. In one year's campaign they were closed in thirty towns and cities — Charlotte, Greensboro, Durham, Goldsboro, Elizabeth City, and New Bern heading the list, with Raleigh, which substituted a dispensary for twenty-four saloons, coming second. As a result of these elections North Carolina stands second best in the United States records of liquor licenses — only one state having fewer in proportion to population. The total number of saloons in the State is about 175 — my records show 162. I count 18 dispensaries in the State, with at least five others in definite prospect. . . .

In conclusion let me remind the reader that the civic treatment of the drink evil can by no means suffice. We must increase the preventive measures of (1) parental exhortation, (2) day school and Sunday school instruction, (3) legal protection of minors, (4) constant exhortation and example against drinking. We must also continue to close the industrial domain to the drinker; not the drunkard, but the drinker. And we must arrive at a more effectual method of treating the drunkard — our most dangerous citizen. I have no special cure to recommend; but I do recommend that, one or more cures having been tried in vain, the State shall take charge of him and protect the society which he menaces, not to mention his more immediate need of protection from himself. There are drunkards not a few who are more dangerous than maniacs. The last testimony of the average victim of the gallows is that drink incited him to murder. To let such men go unrestrained is wholly unworthy of a civilized people.

JOHN E. WHITE

Prohibition: The New Task and Opportunity of the South

1908

Given the later opposition to the Eighteenth Amendment, which provided for national Prohibition between its enactment in 1920 and its repeal in 1933, Bailey's reservations about national and statewide Prohibition were prophetic. But in the years before World War I, people opposed to strong measures of Prohibition remained in a minority among Anti-Saloon League prohibitionists. More typical of sentiment among prohibitionists is this essay written by the Reverend John E. White, a Baptist minister and social reformer in Atlanta.

. . . What is the Prohibition movement? From the standpoint of the sociologist it is a social movement to fix the attitude of social institutions *against* a great social enemy — the Liquor Traffic. From the standpoint of the statesman it is a movement to set the institutions of government *against* a public enemy — the Liquor Traffic. From the standpoint of the publicist it is a movement to put an end to political compromise with a moral iniquity — the Liquor Traffic. This compromise of states with the Liquor Traffic was based originally upon the fear that the Liquor Traffic was politically too strong for the state, and therefore the best course was to make it pay a tribute tax to the state for the privilege of unmolested traffic in the weaknesses of the people of the state.

The Prohibition movement in this new day proposes that society must not smile but frown upon its enemies, that government must minister

John E. White, "Prohibition: The New Task and Opportunity of the South," *South Atlantic Quarterly* 7 (April 1908): 130–42.

positively to the public morality, that the state should have no part with moral evil nor share in its gains, and that the necessity of compromise no longer exists on any ground of fear of the power of the Liquor Traffic.

Now this movement is making tremendous headway all over the country, — echo of it is heard in Europe, — but the main-spring of it is located in the Southern States of North America. In the South it arose in its new significance and power. The South is the propagandic base of the national agitation. The concert of influence in Congress is gathered about Southern representatives. And it is in the South that the main demonstration on such a commanding scale and under such conditions as to afford an object lesson to the whole world.

That the Prohibition movement therefore means something in a large and peculiar way to the civilization of the Southern people, aside from benefits immediate and local, bringing a new and a great task and consequently a new and a great opportunity, is the conviction ventured in this study. . . .

The question of concern to many people who are looking on with some amazement at the immense proportions of the movement in the South is whether society is morally disciplined to sustain it successfully and permanently. Answering that question in the affirmative, let me point out that the issue does not depend on holding to any particular form of Prohibition laws which a State may have started out with. The issue is whether the South is inaugurating a permanent attitude toward the saloon and whether we shall ever return to the old license system.[1] Laws in their detail may undergo amendment in conformity to a general scheme in the Southern States, but the policy of Prohibition as a final treatment of the Liquor Traffic will not be reversed and will sooner or later be written into the fundamental law of each State. This conclusion demands more than a mere assertion. Prohibition will not succeed merely because one might wish it to.

Unquestionably all laws which limit personal action, even for the manifest benefit of society, meet with constant counter currents. The logic of those who insist that such laws require a fixed public sentiment and a preponderating public opinion in their support is sound logic. Unquestionably the contention that tempests of popular enthusiasm,

---

[1] The license system, which was popular around the country in the mid- and late nineteenth century, provided a system by which taverns and saloons were licensed for operation by local and state governments. Temperance reformers and prohibitionists objected to the license system in part because it did not limit the excesses of saloons and in part because it gave governments a stake in their profitability.

however holy in purpose, always sweep back as the tides and leave behind a state of moral fatigue, is a sound contention. These principles have been demonstrated and in no cause more frequently than in temperance reforms. If the Prohibition movement we are now considering were a gift out of hand, or if it were the result of furious upheaval in public sentiment, no amount of ardent protest would avail against the inevitable and disastrous reaction. But in the present situation that which most assures the permanency of a Prohibition policy for the Southern States is just this principle of evolution instead of revolution as the guarantee against revulsion. The difference between me and my Local Option friend who prophesies a return to the saloon system is not a difference in our principles, but over a question of fact as to the soundness and success of the educational process in which the Southern people have been engaged for more than thirty years. The Prohibition movement in Georgia, for instance, has at no stage been a popular enthusiasm. It did not come to power by campaign. There might have been a campaign as there is in North Carolina, but the result was already compounded in social education just as it is in North Carolina. The real moral deed of Prohibition was done without observation. Through steadfast perseverance of years its foundations had been laid. It slowly gained the land. It incorporated itself in community after community, in county after county — till the common social sense covered the State and spoke as the voice of the State. This is the fact explaining what we are now witnessing in the South. At the dawn of 1907 the saloons tolerated in a population of twenty-five million people numbered only half as many as could be found in one single city in the North. Moreover, when Prohibition gained a foothold in counties, it began at once to conquer the hearts of those who originally opposed it. Minorities were educated and absorbed and Prohibition passed out of the arena of controversy with these majorities of Southern people. Look at it. In the States which constituted the old Southern Confederacy there was at the dawn of 1907, out of their total of 994 counties, a preponderant mass of 825 counties which had adopted the Prohibition policy and were in the unchallenged pursuance of it. This was the situation when what is ignorantly called the "Prohibition wave," or the "Prohibition experiment," began to attract general attention by its rapidity of consummation. If the State legislators in the South had met in a congress to represent their constituencies in a vote on Prohibition as a policy, a congress of Senate and House members of the twelve Southern General Assemblies of 1907, the vote would have stood 1,400 to 600 in favor of Prohibition. It was this realized status of the public will that has made the Prohibition movement so easily resistless. Here were these vast majorities; what else could have been natural in a Democracy such as the South is? The immediate advance to State and general Prohibition is simply a normal movement to confirm in law what is already confirmed in social purpose. The momentum of the movement which astonishes the newspapers is the energy that properly accompanies the last blow of a long and patient hammering, the last stroke that sends the confident boat across the line, the last leap in the last lap of the race that wins the goal. The tidal character of the movement, the sense that everything is being borne irresistibly forward, shared by the liquor dealer no less than by the prohibitionist, the disclosure that for years the Liquor Traffic has been resting on a surely thinning crust of popular toleration, the calmness of the public mind toward its dismay and confusion at the disclosure, and the sense of finality in what is being done, which pervades the atmosphere, constitute a phenomenon of the Prohibition movement explainable only and completely by the fact that it is not a revolution but an evolution with roots deep thrust and a life history behind it and vital progress in it.

Another interesting fact in the present progress of Prohibition which differentiates the movement from all former temperance reforms is that in its narrow sense temperance is not its main objective. It is not an effort to make men good by law. Of course it purposes to create conditions which will assist men to be sober who want to be sober and will make it difficult for men to get drunk who want to get drunk. But a study of the controlling motive of public sentiment will reveal that its spirit is mainly what may be characterized as the higher social selfishness. The drunkard and the drunkard's interests are not the chief consideration, though these things are not lost sight of. It is the drinker as a husband, a father, a voter, a worker, a citizen — the man as a social factor, who is being considered. Consequently the movement is marked by an alliance of forces never before enlisted in coöperation against the saloon. It would have been impossible to bring radicals and conservatives together in a fight against inebriety as an individual curse or against whiskey drinking as a wicked personal habit. Almost nothing has been heard of teetotalism. The crank and the fanatic have not controlled its councils. Small emphasis has been heard on the stock appeals to emotion.

The Anti-Saloon League[2] is justly accredited with the wisdom of a new sort of propaganda, and, where the League has elicited, combined and

---

[2] The Anti-Saloon League was founded in Ohio in 1895. By the early 1900s, it had become a national organization and the leading pressure group in favor of Prohibition.

directed public sentiment successfully, the broader program of appeal has been insisted on and adhered to.

The people of the South are the historical partisans of personal liberty. They are naturally opposed to sumptuary laws of any kind. Thousands of men are with the Prohibition movement who have always had whiskey in their homes for personal and domestic use. They have not been aroused and are not aroused against whiskey *per se*. And it has gone contrary to the grain to contemplate as they do the limitation which Prohibition will place upon their personal liberty in that matter. But there they are, and it is the hopefulest sign of Southern civilization that they are there, for it reveals the dawning of a sense of social obligation than which Christianity holds nothing finer for the future of society. They are opposed to the Liquor Traffic, opposed to its investment of millions of dollars in a demoralizing social agency, opposed to its cold blooded attitude toward humanity, its essential lack of patriotism, its interference with industrial efficiency, its consistent alliance with crime and every evil, its necessary antagonism to all the agencies of character building, and to its particular peril to the peace and happiness of the South, which has the great problem of the races on its hands. In short, the intelligent people of the South are looking upon Prohibition, not as a temperance reform, but as statesmanship — a public policy, favorable to religion, favorable to education, favorable to industry, favorable to the coming generation, and as a necessity of Southern conditions in particular, and as an ideal of social obligation to a broad general good.

Where these considerations have never been so formulated, and with men who could not formulate such an explanation of their attitude toward the Prohibition movement, they are the real considerations felt with varying degrees of earnestness throughout the rank of Southern society.

In addition to the steady development of the anti-saloon conviction in the South, upon which Prohibition depends, there are conditions not found elsewhere which have contributed to its popular appeal and stand stoutly in support of its permanency. One of these conditions, in the judgment of some, is the probable explanation of the general attitude of the Southern people. I refer to the race question — the presence of eight million negroes.

The feeling of insecurity in the rural sections of the South on account of vagrant and drunken negroes had become a contagion among the country women. A little of this sort of thing goes a long way in the South. Public sentiment has become intensely stimulated by it. Probably no demonstration under Prohibition will be calculated to make a more influential impression on the country people than to show them an end to drunken negro parties, the return from the nearby towns, and the courts uncongested by negro cases.

But more than this in real importance, for several years two ideas have been growing strong in the intelligence of the South, both of which have force in bringing on and fixing Prohibition as a settled policy.

The fact that the negro constitutes a child-people element in our population, that the great mass of the negroes are ignorant and weak and therefore are to be thought for in government and protected from the perils of liberty, is an ascending idea in the legislative scheme of the South. The moral basis of the disfranchisement movement was this: thousands of the best men — the justest men — went with this movement in consideration of the true welfare of the negro race, their thought being that through such limitation only could the discipline of citizenship become possible. This idea of the negro is more pronounced in the Prohibition movement. It stands out more nobly. The saloon was the ravager of the negro people. It plundered them at all points, robbed them of their wages, fed their animalism, and was, as every one knows, a debauching agent let loose by law upon them.

Another fact made constantly more prominent in the South's study of herself is a condition among a considerable mass of the white population not entirely unlike the condition among the negroes — ignorance, poverty, and irresponsibility. This constitutes the other half of the race peril. The new movement in public education has made clear this fact as one to be seriously reckoned with. There are these thousands — should we say millions? — of our own Anglo-Saxon stock, not yet raised to a safe level of civilization, not yet, by education and opportunity, strong enough to reckon their social responsibility and to resist the elemental impulse of lawlessness, when racial antipathies are aroused. The obligation of a democracy to make law minister to their development is being felt more and more in the South and has a place in the interpretation of the Prohibition policy.

These are the two elements of Southern society that define the acute dangers of the race problem. It is realized that in any Southern community with a bar-room a race war is a perilously possible occurrence. The danger is not in the upper but in the lower levels of both races. There the inflammable fringes hang loose. Following the racial lines from top to bottom, it became evident to everybody that the lines of both races converged at the saloon, which stood at the acute angle of the inverted social pyramid. It was the attractive social center for the dangerous elements of our population.

At their hearts the intelligent white people of the South are sick of the race issue as a menace to social peace. They are tired of the depraved and criminal negro. They are tired of the irresponsible white man. The Liquor Traffic fostered and encouraged both. I say, therefore, that the negro is not the only nor the chief reason for Prohibition in the South, and yet its permanency as a policy will find always a ready and powerful justification in the fact that there are eight million negroes in the South, constituting the most difficult sociological problem any people ever had, which the Liquor Traffic only tended to complicate. . . .

Our recent history has been forcing to the front, and in such a way that the matter was unavoidable, that the South as a section and the Southern people as a people were to be brought in some serious way to consider their civilization imperilled by a lawless spirit. It is not necessary here to explain how the Southern white people were forced into an attitude toward the National Constitution that gave us thirty years' training away from love of law as such. It is a fact to be taken into large account when we are explaining lawlessness in the South. But for some time public attention has been turning strongly the other way, to the fact that the question of law, the necessity of doing things by law, is imperative. The disfranchisement of the negro by law was the first great result of this return of social reason in the South. Having accomplished that, we cannot stop there. Having accomplished that, the white people have now to consider themselves. This is their civilization. It is what they are. It will be what they become. So I repeat, the trend of attention has been forced toward a realized weakness of our civilization in respect of law. There is a hopeful change of tone toward the statistics of lawlessness which show the South at a disadvantage as compared with the rest of the country — even the disorderly new civilization of the West. Our newspapers now publish them without that sort of comment that kills public conscience. They show the record of the South a sorrowful one, though for 1907 we are now rejoicing that our people were guilty of only fifty out of fifty-six lynchings in the United States as against sixty-seven out of seventy-three in 1906.

Now Prohibition presents this grave question with a new issue. Heretofore discussions of lawlessness have been chiefly in relation to the absorbing problem of the negro. The sacredness of law was put almost always in conflict with shocking crimes. The best citizenship of the South, therefore, had not been able to make more than a stifled protest for law.

But Prohibition offers an issue of favorable conditions for lining up the moral and patriotic elements of Southern society on the side of law. The task is laid on us to prove that we are strong enough in civilization to constrain men or compel them to honor laws whether they are pleased with them or not. That is one test to which the Prohibition policy will submit the South.

The other issue is the integrity of democracy. In a democracy, when the people are evenly divided on any great proposition, anarchy always lurks near. Democratic government is most secure in the normal nature of things when majorities are pronounced. But the question arises in connection with the Prohibition policy in the Southern States, whether our democracy is secure, if a weak minority can prevent the will of the people and defeat the execution of their will expressed in legislation. Look at the situation as it is in Georgia. The majority demanding the prohibition of the Liquor Traffic is immense. This is not disputed. Can the people of Georgia sustain their will? Is there not here an issue going to the foundations of democracy? It is not a question of the small and unusual violations of the Prohibition law, as in the case of all other laws against crime, occurring in the ordinary experience of its execution. It is a question of considerable bodies of citizens in determined desire to see the will of the people overthrown lawlessly. If the people of a State, representing an overwhelming majority of citizenship, cannot have what they legally have chosen to have, the failure is more than a failure of Prohibition. It is the breaking down of democracy. It would not be a failure of democracy, of course, but its vindication, if those opposed to Prohibition as a policy of the State should seek by appointed means to change its majority to a minority and get rid of it by repeal; but we are not about to meet an honest, open, patriotic effort of this kind, but a lawless, unscrupulous resistance to the Prohibition law by two classes — the criminal and the anti-Prohibitionist element which encourages the criminal by moral support.

The point, then, is this: The battle for democracy and law is coming on in the South over the Prohibition issue. It ought to be made an aggressive and uncompromising battle. Therefore the real issues of it should not lack for strong emphasis.

The South needs this struggle. Those who desire the civilization of the South to be a law-loving, democracy-loving civilization are called on to make it a triumphant struggle. The lines should be, and I believe will be, drawn sharply. The division is to be made and the issue joined between those who are in favor of the honest and successful execution of the Prohibition law for the two reasons that it is the law and that the people will it, and those who resist the law and violate it, and with them those who shield and excuse and wink at its violation because they are personally opposed to Prohibition.

The South has much to gain from such a conflict. It would mean a great progress. It is to be prayed that we are going into it really, that a great spirit may be aroused, a great agitation drawn on. The next quarter century ought to see in every State, possibly in every local and county campaign, a political excitement over the question of the Prohibition policy. Through such training we would come to an alliance of conscience on all the South's problems.

The Prohibition issue, as the issue of law and democracy, is the task and the opportunity — the wide opportunity of the South. It is the opportunity to get together and into organized relations the intelligence and moral conscience of the Southern people — for this and other causes. It is the opportunity to lessen greatly the unhealthy attention to the negro question, which has absorbed Southern thought to our hurt for so long. It is the opportunity to emphasize our recognition of the South's responsibility for the negro's moral welfare. Anglo-Saxon supremacy should thus be exercised in consideration of our kindly concern about his development in our midst. It is the opportunity to achieve a real leadership in the nation by example, by assistance to the Prohibition movements in other sections, and by influence in national legislation on the subject. It is the opportunity — the first since the civil war — to play a part distinctly, of noble proportions, in the moral progress of humanity at large, by the demonstration that a grand division of Anglo-Saxon States can meet and master a problem that has always overmastered Anglo-Saxon people even in their oldest civilization; for the Drink Traffic curse is a world problem. . . .

BOOKER T. WASHINGTON

Prohibition and the Negro

1908

Support for Prohibition was strong, perhaps the strongest of any of the Progressive Era social reforms. As this document suggests, the Prohibition movement — as well as other social reforms — crossed racial lines. Although John E. White and other white prohibitionists suggested Prohibition as a measure of racial control, significant support grew among black reformers. This article, by the most influential African American leader of his time, Booker T. Washington (1856–1915), offers reasons why blacks might endorse Prohibition.

What are the results of two months of prohibition in two large Southern cities, Atlanta, Georgia, and Birmingham, Alabama? The answer to this question contains some very interesting facts. It will be recalled that on the first of January of this year all the bar-rooms in Atlanta, Georgia, and throughout the State for that matter, and all the bar-rooms in the city of Birmingham, Alabama, were closed. Of course two months is too short a time in which to draw definite and permanent conclusions, but nevertheless this period emphasizes some valuable lessons.

I have read much in the Northern papers about the prohibition movement in the South being based wholly upon a determination or desire to keep liquor away from the negroes and at the same time provide a way for the white people to get it. I have watched the prohibition movement carefully from its inception to the present time, and I have seen nothing in the agitation in favor of the movement, nothing in the law itself, and nothing in the execution of the law that warrants any such conclusion. The prohibition movement is based upon a deep-seated desire to get rid of whisky in the interest of both races because of its hurtful economic and moral results. The prohibition sentiment is as strong in counties where there are practically no colored people as in the Black Belt counties.

If I mention these facts here, by way of introduction to what I have to say in regard to the results of prohibition where I have been able to observe them, namely, two typical Southern cities, Birmingham and Atlanta, it is because I want to emphasize the fact that the contrary is true:

Booker T. Washington, "Prohibition and the Negro," *Outlook* 88 (Mar. 14, 1908): 587–89.

prohibition in the South is essentially a moral movement, the first effect of which has been a remarkable reduction in crime. Putting it roundly, according to the reports of the police magistrates, prohibition has reduced the amount of crime in Birmingham one-third and in Atlanta one-half, since January 1, when the law went into force.

The significance of these facts will be appreciated when you consider the extraordinary number of people who are arrested and sent to the mines and penitentiaries every year by the criminal courts of these two cities. During the year 1907 the police of Atlanta, according to a report in the Atlanta Constitution of January 1, made 24,332 arrests. This means that during the year, on an average, one person out of every six in the city of Atlanta was arrested. And this number has been increasing. There were 2,630 more persons arrested in 1907 than in 1906. This is an increase of considerably more than twelve per cent in one year.

Of course this does not mean that one person in every six in Atlanta is a criminal, because a good many persons represented in these statistics were arrested several times during the year, and a good many others were arrested but not convicted. Putting the best construction upon the facts, however, they indicate an abnormal drain upon the ranks of the peaceful and law-abiding people of the city into the classes that fill the penitentiaries and supply recruits to the chain-gangs, which are already doing too large a portion of the work of the State. It should be taken into account also that, under present conditions, Southern prisons are conducted too largely for the purpose of punishing men rather than reforming them, and they are therefore constantly discharging back into the ranks of the industrious and law-abiding populations a stream of hardened and embittered men and women, which in turn pollutes the masses of the people with which it mingles.

Prohibition has attacked this evil at its source, and the results which the enforcement of this law brought about serve to indicate to what extent evils that the South has accepted as human and inevitable can be modified and cured, if proper measures are taken and these measures are backed by the will of the people.

In his report to the Mayor at the end of the first month of prohibition, Judge N. B. Feagin, of Birmingham, makes the following statement:

"The decrease in arrests average about as follows, in comparing January, 1908, under prohibition with January, 1907, with saloons: Aggregate arrests, decrease 33⅓ per cent; for assault with intent to murder, 22 per cent; gambling, 17 per cent; drunkenness, 80 per cent; disorderly conduct, 35 per cent; burglary and grand larceny, 33 per cent; vagrancy, 40 per cent; wife-beating, 70 per cent."

There were 33 arrests for drunkenness in January, 1908, as against 174 for the same month of 1907. There were 56 arrests for disorderly conduct in January, 1908, as against 90 for the same month of 1907.

Several times during the past eight weeks there has not been a single prisoner before the Recorder's Court at Atlanta charged with drunkenness. The first instance of this kind was January 4, when there were but 17 cases on the docket; nine of these were cases of children. On the same day a year before 63 cases were tried in that court, of which 32 were for drunkenness and 28 for disorderly conduct. Wednesday, January 29, at the session of what was called by the local papers "the smallest police court ever held," there was only one prisoner at the morning session. It was about this time that the newspapers recorded another extraordinary event in the history of the city. For the first time in many years, the jail was for several days empty.

The records of arrests for the month of January show a more extraordinary decrease in Atlanta than in Birmingham. For the month of January, 1907, 1,653 cases were put on the docket of the Recorder's Court in Atlanta. During the month of January, 1908, on the other hand, there were but 768 cases on the docket, a decrease of considerably more than 50 per cent. During January, 1907, there were 341 cases of drunkenness tried, but in 1908 only 64, a decrease of more than 80 per cent.

The Justices of the Peace, before whom warrants in minor criminal cases are issued, report a similar falling off. Three classes of warrants ordinarily taken out by negroes and the poorer class of whites show, according to reports in the newspapers, a falling off equal to that of the Recorder's Court. These are the warrants charging abandonment of minor children, dispossessory warrants — taken against people unable to pay their rents — and warrants charging various kinds of larceny. A good many of these cases grow out of family quarrels, and serve as a sort of barometer of the condition among the poorer classes in the city. These evidences indicate that the closing of the saloons and the breeding-places of crimes and disorders has brought a remarkable change into the homes of the poor, where, finally, the effects of crime and disorder are always most keenly felt.

Commenting on the situation as it is in Atlanta and Birmingham, the Birmingham News says: "For ten years Birmingham has not enjoyed so orderly a period as it has since the 1st of January. The moral improvement in the city has been marked since prohibition went into effect. The newspapers are no longer giving space to reports of murders, shooting and cutting scrapes, personal altercations and other disorders, as they formerly did, for the reason that the regard for law and order in this community is very much more in evidence since the removal of the whisky traffic."

In Birmingham the demand for reform has not stopped with the closing of the saloons. Since January 1 seventeen gambling-houses, many of which had been running for years in a more or less public way, have been closed. A Law and Order League has been formed, and vigorous measures are being taken throughout Jefferson County to do away with the "blind tigers"[1] and to suppress the vices that have centered about and in these moral cesspools.

The interesting thing about the prohibition movement in the South is that it goes out from and is supported by the churches. The campaign in Jefferson County, Alabama, which changed Birmingham from wet to dry began, as I have been informed, in a ministers' meeting. The superintendent of the Anti-Saloon League in Alabama, Mr. Brooks Lawrence, is a minister and a Northerner. One of the charges brought against him during the campaign was that he was a carpetbagger, and that the prohibition movement was an attempt "to dump Northern ideas" upon the South, where they did not fit conditions.

It was predicted that prohibition would demoralize business. In Birmingham alone one hundred and twenty-eight saloons, fourteen wholesale liquor stores, and two breweries were closed as a result of the law. But the predictions do not seem to have been fulfilled. It has recently been announced that a fourteen-story building was to be erected on the site of one of the oldest saloons in Birmingham; and Atlanta is preparing to pave and improve the notorious Decatur Street, on which the larger part of the dives of the city were located. It is promised that it will soon become one of the best streets in the city.

Prohibition has been the popular issue, and it has the South behind it. Many of those, I am informed, who voted for prohibition were men who themselves belonged to the class that has supported the saloon. On the other hand, many of those who opposed prohibition were men who rarely, if ever, entered a bar-room.

Directly and indirectly, the members of my own race have suffered, perhaps more than any other portion of the population, from the effects of the liquor traffic. But the educated men and the leaders of the race have been quick to see the advantages that would come from the total suppression of the saloon. Everywhere in the South this class have given their votes to the support of prohibition even where it brought them in opposition to the men whom they have been disposed to regard as their friends,

[1] Illegally operating saloons.

in the support of those whom they have been accustomed to regard as their enemies. In Birmingham the negroes formed an organization, and cast nearly all of the registered colored vote for prohibition.

Prohibition in the South is to a certain extent a woman's movement. In the campaign in Alabama it was the women, the mothers and the wives and the children of the men who supported the saloon with their earnings, who marched in the processions, and stood all day at the polls to see that their husbands, sons, and fathers voted "right."

No one who is at all acquainted with the conditions in the South can doubt the depth and the genuineness of the feelings that are behind prohibition in the South, which is in no way a political maneuver, but an inspired movement of the masses of the people. Its great importance, it seems to me, consists in the fact that it is bringing the ordinary conservative elements in the community, the women, the ministers, and the people in the churches, into close and intimate contact with actual conditions and with the real problems of the South. It is at the same time, if I may say so, an intellectual awakening and a moral revolution.

4

Child Labor

Deeply concerned about children, Progressive Era social reformers focused many of their reform efforts on what contemporaries have called child-saving — seeking to protect, nurture, and preserve the child from the harsh realities of everyday life. The Progressive Era marked the emergence of a new conception of the role of children in society. Prior to the twentieth century, children served as an important source of labor; large families were essential on the farm, and boys and girls by the age of twelve performed important tasks. Children spent less time in school than at work; before 1900, the average American boy or girl attended school less than six months per year.

Far from changing the child-labor economy, the industrial revolution in the South expanded the use of children in mills and factories. During and after the 1890s, as southern cotton mills underwent a period of rapid growth and expansion, mill owners blanketed the villages and farms of the rural Piedmont area that stretched from Virginia to Mississippi with recruiting agents. These agents arrived armed with descriptions of mill towns and factories that offered high wages and secure employment, and they promised that farm families could migrate and work as family units. Insofar as was possible, the workers themselves wanted to preserve their rural traditions. They lived in "mill villages" — company-owned houses near the cotton textile factories — and these communities usually had the appearance of rural hamlets. Not surprisingly, millworkers, as they had on the farm, worked as families — and the industrial workforce included men, women, and children. While their mothers and fathers worked full-time in the mill, young children often performed odd jobs and worked as "helpers"; in this fashion, the mill provided day care for mill children. In 1900, one-quarter of all workers in southern cotton mills were between the ages of ten and sixteen, and in some sectors of the textile industry, the proportion of child workers was even higher.

By the time children reached the age of twelve, they were already fully acclimated to the culture of the mill, where they were expected to work long hours — usually more than sixty hours per week — for low wages and where they could be employed in night shifts. Laboring under the same unsafe conditions existing for most early-twentieth-century Americans, southern child workers faced the constant threat of injury, dismemberment, and death. They worked under the deafeningly loud noise of the power spinning and weaving machines. They also experienced the more subtle threat of the lung disease lyssinosia ("brown lung" disease), which was caused by exposure to the cotton dust that filled mill air. Because they went to work at an early age, child laborers spent little time in school, with a resulting illiteracy rate three or four times greater than that among southern children not working in mills.

In the Progressive Era, the attitudes of social reformers contrasted with that prevailing among most of the members of the southern mill community. Reformers believed that, instead of thrusting children into the workplace, parents should protect them from the pressures of work. The proper place for the socialization of children, Progressive reformers passionately believed, was the school rather than the factory. The rise of child psychology, which had emerged as an academic discipline of study, buttressed these new attitudes: Childhood and adolescence were special periods of growth during which the adult personality was formed. Many social reformers believed that children should be "saved" from early exposure to work. The most important issue among Americans, declared one reformer, was the "physical, the intellectual, the moral, and the spiritual good of the children." The "boy of today," concluded another reformer, would become "the man of tomorrow." Children were "plastic, impressionable, aspiring, and recurring," and if reformers could solve the problems at childhood, "you have solved all social problems."[1]

The efforts of southern social reformers to legislate an end to the use of younger children in southern textile mills grew out of their belief in the need to save children from their environment. Labor unions such as the American Federation of Labor (AFL), led by President Samuel Gompers, had long supported the passage of legislation that would have made the employment of children in industry illegal. In 1900–1901, Gompers and the AFL hired a young aristocratic Englishwoman, Irene M. Ashby, to tour southern mills and to report the extent of child labor in the southern textile industry. Efforts by Ashby (see p. 87) and other reformers resulted in the exposure of conditions to the public. In Alabama, Ashby made contact with a young Episcopal minister, Edgar Gardner Murphy, and he

---

[1] Quoted in William A. Link, *The Paradox of Southern Progressivism, 1880–1930* (Chapel Hill: University of North Carolina, 1992), 162.

and other ministers in the state capital, Montgomery, organized the Alabama Child Labor Committee, which was composed of ministers, women's clubs members, and other reformers, to campaign for new laws to restrict the use of child workers. The efforts of Murphy and other Alabama reformers enjoyed limited success: In 1903, the state legislature enacted legislation setting a minimum age of twelve for industrial labor, but the law was accompanied by so many exemptions that effective restriction did not exist. Meanwhile, similar campaigns emerged across much of the rest of the cotton textile South. In North Carolina, the Presbyterian minister and editor Alexander J. McKelway led a campaign for strong legislation, although the legislature in 1903 enacted a law no stronger than that passed in Alabama. In the same year in South Carolina, labor unions, some of the state's newspapers, and the important women's group the King's Daughters of Columbia, South Carolina, passed legislation restricting work to children over the age of twelve.

These efforts at campaigns to enact restrictive legislation in the textile South had obvious limitations, and the failure of efforts to regulate child labor played an important role in the organization of the National Child Labor Committee (NCLC) in April 1904. The NCLC, a national organization, was dedicated to ending the use of children as workers across the United States. But much of its effort soon became focused on the South, and many of its important leaders came out of the early child-labor campaigns in the South. Edgar Gardner Murphy served as the secretary of the NCLC soon after its formation, and in 1904 he was chiefly responsible for the hiring of the North Carolina child-labor reformer Alexander J. McKelway as the director of the committee's efforts in the South (see the McKelway document, p. 97).

After joining the NCLC in 1904, McKelway orchestrated a continuing effort to enact new laws and to strengthen existing ones regarding the use of children as workers. In 1905, McKelway conducted an energetic campaign in North Carolina to raise the age limit of girls working in industry from twelve to fourteen, to impose for children a maximum of sixty hours per week, and to raise the working age to sixteen for workers employed in night shifts. But in North Carolina and elsewhere, the NCLC campaign encountered strong opposition, from both mill owners and mill parents. Although by 1910 all of the industrial South had established minimum ages for employment, the laws were largely unsuccessful. Even those legislatures that passed laws regulating the working conditions of children failed to provide any effective way in which the law could be enforced.

The failure to make significant changes in the conditions of working children had two significant effects. First, the NCLC after 1910 began more direct efforts to expose and publicize the continuing extent of child labor. The committee dispatched special investigators directly responsible to its national offices, and they reported regular, even systematic, violations of the weak laws limiting working by children in mills. Particularly effective in documenting the widespread problem of child labor were the investigations of Lewis W. Hine (see p. 105), a photojournalist who worked for the NCLC and investigated child labor in the textile mills and canneries of the South. Second, lacking faith in the ability of the South to solve the problem of child labor locally, the NCLC began a campaign in 1914 to persuade Congress to intervene, and in 1916 it enacted the first national child-labor law.

Child-labor reform was an important, perhaps even central, part of southern Progressivism. When reading the documents in this chapter, consider the following questions:

1. How do the views of Ashby and McKelway resemble those of Walter Hines Page in his "Rebuilding of Old Commonwealths"? What values and assumptions do they share? On what points do they differ?

2. What attitudes does each reformer exhibit toward the industrial mill community? How do they view workers? To what extent are they patronizing and paternalistic? To what extent are they sympathetic with that culture?

3. How much evidence appears in the documents about how the mill community viewed these reformers?

4. What do Ashby and McKelway see as the most important cause of the problem of child labor? What do they see as the best way to solve this problem?

5. How do the photographs of Lewis W. Hine complement the investigations of Ashby and McKelway? To what kind of audience do the photographs appeal?

IRENE M. ASHBY

Child-Labor in Southern Cotton Mills

1901

Irene M. Ashby provides one reformer's view of child labor in the southern textile industry. In 1900, Ashby traveled to the United States from her native England. She had been a young woman of established social standing living a "life of garden parties, theaters, and balls," Ashby recalled, when she discovered social reform. Convinced that the only way to help the masses was to live with them, she worked in the West London Social Guild, a settlement house. Suffering from poor health, she traveled to the United States, where she sought out American Federation of Labor president Samuel F. Gompers. When she asked Gompers if she could serve as a labor organizer, he instead suggested that she tour the South to promote legislation restricting the use of child labor. Investigating some twenty-five mills in Alabama as well as touring other states in the textile South, Ashby made a strong impression among southern reformers, especially women. One Atlanta reformer remembered Ashby as a "blond and fair and petite" woman whose blue eyes were "steady." Part of a "great and growing class of young men and women" who were attracted to social service, Ashby reports here on her findings in southern mills.

The South now has nearly seven hundred cotton mills, one hundred and thirteen of which were built in 1899 alone. Such rapid progress cannot take place without producing unnatural conditions of some sort. The worst evil that has come with this rapid growth of cotton mills it needs no expert to discover. It is the same evil that the cotton manufacturing towns of England and of New England suffered, and against which a long and strenuous agitation was necessary.

Come with me to an Alabama town, where there is a large cheerful-looking factory. Walking up the long, orderly building, deafened by the racket, yet fascinated by the ingenious machinery, you become suddenly aware of a little gray shadow flitting restlessly up and down the aisles — a small girl, and with bare feet and pale face. She has a worn and anxious aspect, as if a weight of care and responsibility rested already on her baby

Irene M. Ashby, "Child-Labor in Southern Cotton Mills," *World's Work* 2 (Oct. 1901): 1290–95.

shoulders. She either does not look at you at all or she turns her eyes but for a moment, unchildlike in their lack of interest, looking back immediately to the spinning frame. A thread breaks first at one end of the long frame, then at the other. The tiny fingers repair the damage at the first place and she walks listlessly to the other. Something goes wrong above, and the child pushes forward a box to stand on that she may reach it. With a great shock it dawns on you that this child is working.

This is a scene with which I became too painfully familiar ever to forget or to misrepresent. During the latter half of December, 1900, and the first half of January, 1901, I visited twenty-four cotton mills in sixteen cities and villages of Alabama. I chose Alabama because the industry, although comparatively new there (only four out of the twenty-four mills I went through averaging more than five years' existence), is in an active stage of growth, and a child-labor bill had been pending before the Legislature.

I was prepared to find child-labor, for wherever easily manipulated machinery takes the place of human muscles the child is inevitably drawn into the labor market, unless there are laws to protect it. But one could hardly be prepared to find in America today white children, six and seven years of age, working for twelve hours a day — aroused before daybreak and toiling till long after sundown in winter, with only half an hour for rest and refreshment. When the mills are tempted by pressure of work they make the same old mistakes of their industrial ancestry. Some of them run the machinery at night, and little children are called on to endure the strain of all-night work — and are sometimes kept awake by the vigilant superintendent with cold water dashed into their faces. I should hardly have believed it had I not seen these things myself.

One evening in December I stumbled through a totally unlighted mill village, falling by the way into ditches and deep ruts, and knocked at the door of one of the wooden huts where I saw a light. I asked the woman who opened it if I might come in. Assenting, she ushered me in. She was surrounded by a brood of very small boys, and her consumptive husband sat beside the fire. The smallest child, a poor little fellow that looked to be about six years old, nestled up to me as I talked to them. All worked in the mill, except the mother, they told me.

"Not this one!" I exclaimed, looking down at the wee, thin boy beside me.

"Why, yes." He had worked for about a year; last year he worked forty nights; he was nearly eight years old now. They left that mill because the night work was too hard on the children.

In answer to a query from me, the child said that he could scarcely sleep at all in the day time.

At one place I heard of children, working on the night shift, turned out for some fault at two o'clock in the morning, allowed by a compassionate clerk to go to sleep on a bench in the office, as they were afraid to go home. Ladies told me, too, of a common sight in the mill cottages: children lying face downward on the bed sleeping with exhaustion, just as they had come in from the night shift, too utterly weary even to remove their clothes.

The long day work for children prevailed in every mill that I visited: in six of these night work had been or was still the custom.

This problem is not a new one. It has had to be faced in every place where textile trades have been established. But the Southern States now enjoy the unenviable position of being the only civilized country in the world which does not by enlightened legislation protect the chilren of its working people from this inevitable consequence of unregulated industrial development.

In Europe — England, France, Germany, Italy, Holland, Belgium, Switzerland, Denmark, Sweden, and even Russia — there are laws prohibiting the employment of children in factories under a minimum age, only Italy placing this lower than twelve years. Most countries insist on at least a small educational qualification and regulate conditions and hours of employment for minors, and limit such employment to the day time. These laws were made necessary by the appalling consequences of leaving the matter alone. Cotton spinners grew rich in England at the beginning of the nineteenth century out of the labor of little children. Had it not been for the check of factory laws, the trade would soon have been wholly worked by women and children, as all possible skill was turned to adapting machinery to their powers. Ring spinning was invented in the United States when male labor to run "the mule" spinning machines was scarce in New England some sixty years ago. In every British colony where manufactures are carried on and in twenty-one States of the Union (including all the northern cotton manufacturing States) legislation has been found imperative. For it has been proved to be perilous to the community for a comparatively small set of mill owners or stockholders and superintendents to procure labor unchecked. They have everywhere done so at the expense of the health, the morals, and the education of a great industrial class. In face of this universal experience it is strange to find the primitive condition of things in the South side by side with the finest modern machinery. Of the mill managers some are, and others affect to be, lamentably ignorant of the history of their own trade; they oppose legislation; some of them have told me that they had no idea that any laws on the subject were in force in the United States.

They have a set of excuses and reasons for child-labor which I found interesting at first, but which I have since heard brought forward so unvaryingly and frequently that they became sad as well as monotonous. Some of these are exceedingly plausible.

We are told that the operatives are far better off in the mills than they have ever been before. It is a pity of course that necessity impels the parents to let their children work, but such work is a grade higher than existence on the country farms.

In a sense this is true: many of them are raw country folk of a low grade who have come from scattered farms, on which they made but a bare living, subsisting by mortgaging next year's cotton-bale for this year's food. Their homes were mere shanties, where they lived with the numerous progeny in one room, knowing not the chink of dollars and cents, unkempt and often addicted to the snuff habit. As mill operatives, their homes are at least an improvement on the shanties; their earnings as a family are fairly good (although the individual wages are small, varying from 10 cents to 30 cents for a child, 50 cents to $1 for a woman, and 65 cents to $1 for a man, a day); unheard-of luxuries, such as lace curtains and a bank account, were cited to me as indications of their bettered condition.

One mill manager kindly took me for a beautiful drive into the country to show me the miserable dwellings of the class from which he drew his mill operatives. Bad enough surely is the life of these shanty-children in the country; but I saw clearly enough to note their rounded limbs and the flush of health in their cheeks, in contrast with the wan and aged look of the mill babies; and I reflected that lace curtains are a poor exchange for children's lives.

I listened to the glowing accounts of the wealth this industry was bringing to Alabama, of the increased value of farm produce and farm labor, of the benefits to trade from the growing needs of the operatives, and I realized that the one class never thought of was the helpless little children whom their parents were sacrificing for momentary prosperity, and who were being injured by the very industry which should be their greatest blessing. Properly regulated, the factory is an immense improvement on the isolated farm, for it brings the people into association with others. But unregulated, no! The children become the victims.

Again, the laziness and general worthlessness of the parents are cited — in proof of which grown men, whittling on the stoop, would be pointed out to me, while children and wives were in the mills. Some are undoubtedly lazy, but they have often been forced by circumstances into an acquiescence which has degenerated into complacency. They come from the country lured by reports of free schools and unlimited work. On arrival at the village they have either been obliged to sign a contract promising the work of four or five members of their family before they are allowed to rent a cottage, or the children have, from the sheer pressure of the habit of the place, gone into the mill. Three little ones count more than one father and are given a heartier welcome. As the rents of their cottages are suited to their low wages, other dwellings in the vicinity — if there are any — are impracticable.

Often the whole family, except the baby actually in the cradle, is in the mill. Two or three of eight years or older might be on the pay-roll, but the youngest paid worker can get through her "side" — at ten cents a day — with more ease if she has her little brother of six to help her. I have seen a boy under four beginning his life of drudgery by pulling the yarn off bobbins to make bands. A manager courteously conducting me through the mill would often explain — at some exclamation from me — "These very little ones are not working; they are only helping their brothers and sisters." I accepted the explanation until it dawned on me how numerous were these wee unpaid assistants. It is a biting comment on the dehumanizing nature of competition that generally kind-hearted and humane men should be willing to profit by the labor of little children — without even a wage return for their work.

The frequent plea that the people would starve were it not for their children's earnings is untrue. In the first place the child seldom earns even its own food and clothes, and several intelligent operatives who had had children in the mill told me that anything these earned was so discounted by ill health that they had taken them out. It is a well established economic fact that the family wage is not increased by child-labor. If the law forbids the working of the children, the older members of the family must be able to earn enough to support the younger. In time the family wage is actually lessened by child-labor, for the standard of health, education, and needs are lowered. In arguments bearing on the hardships to individuals of stopping child-labor, "the poor widow" bulks large. One's anxiety for the poor widow diminishes when one finds that she is made the excuse in every country for retaining child-labor, and that when investigation is made, her contribution in the shape of baby laborers is about two per cent. (as recently shown in England).

In spite of the excellent system of ventilation adopted in most of these factories, by which the atmosphere is rendered bearable, a very little inquiry shows that it is by no means as healthy as one would be led to believe from the eulogies of those who are seldom in it. The flying lint often brings on throat and lung trouble, while pneumonia resulting from the sudden change from the hot factory to the early morning and the late evening mists is not uncommon. These conditions tell far more frequently and fatally on the unformed constitutions of children than on the grown workers. In one factory I found a little girl aged ten, in the "drawing in" room, where every individual thread of the warp is drawn through the "harness" of the weaving loom. She could earn as much sometimes as 75 cents a day, though alas, at the expense of the beautiful blue eyes she turned up to me as I spoke to her. Her mother told me that she brought her youngest daughter, aged seven, into the mill with her, and although urged to allow her to work, there being many as small in the mill, she would not allow it. Yet without doing any work the child had lost in weight in a year through confinement in the mill atmosphere. Over and over again I was told that the mill was a "playground."

"If anyone tells you that," said a superintendent to me with concentrated scorn, "he either doesn't know what he's talking about, or he's telling a downright lie. I've been in the mill since I was eight years old myself, and I know. We're no charity institution."

"What do you do when you are very tired?" I asked a little girl, putting my mouth close to her ear to make myself heard. "I cry," she said, shyly. She would make no reply when I asked her what happened then, but another child, who had literally poked her head into the conversation, put in tersely, "The boss tells her to go on with her work."

There is a difference in the attitude of the managers and of the practical superintendents towards the question of legislation. Many of the latter are secretly in favor of it. They are in contact with the children all day long. Children need a great deal of supervision and are often wasteful workers. When questioned closely almost all acknowledged that those under twelve are more detrimental than helpful as workers.

The strongest objection to preventive legislation is, of course, the desire for cheap labor. To the shame of the Northern capitalist be it said, he has carefully fostered this superstition in order to obtain the cheap and submissive labor that he believes children give. In 1887 a law was passed in Alabama limiting the hours of children's work in factories to eight a day. At the instigation of Massachusetts mill-owners this law was repealed in December, 1894, on their promise that these mill-owners would establish a factory in Alabama. Today the mills thus established are working at least fifty children under twelve years old for eleven and three-quarters hours a day. It is difficult to see the exact benefit to Alabama since all the capital in the Alabama City mills is northern and eastern, and the dividends go out of the State. The village is a beautiful one, managed with much moral and sanitary severity, but no seeming philanthropies, such as natatoriums, churches, and libraries (for people who cannot even read), can atone for this deliberate demoralization of the Southern conscience and injury to the future of her industries by those who in their own State are forbidden to work children by the best factory laws in the world. In Massachusetts no child may go into the mills under fourteen, and only then after having attended school for at least a year.

This is not an isolated instance. Much of the opposition to the passage of a protective law through the Southern legislatures is made by the representatives of Northern corporations, who are taking full advantage of the possibility of child-labor. In eleven mills I visited, owned by Northern capital, there were twice as many children under twelve as in thirteen owned by Southern capital. The total number of children under twelve in the mills of Alabama (including the unpaid "helpers") I computed to be about 1,200. This number is not stationary or diminishing; on the contrary, it is steadily increasing, and the experience of the other Southern States proves that it must be so. In one of the older mills, they told me that the children were younger and more numerous than they had ever had them before. This question has a graver complication in Alabama and throughout the South than it has had in any other part of the world. It is inseparably connected with the color problem. The peril of coming illiterate generations, which confronted Massachusetts in 1870, from the same cause of child-labor, faces the Southern States, and threatens at the same time the supremacy of the white laboring classes over the colored. This rapidly growing mill population is entirely composed of white people. As a correspondent wrote to Labor Commissioner Lacy in North Carolina: "The illiterate negro sends his child to school; the illiterate white man sends his into the cotton mill." In most of the Southern States an educational test for voting is either in force or inevitable in the near future. The white man, to whom the test is not applied, has not the stimulus that the negro has to learn to read. This aspect of the question alone would lift it out of the region of purely economic or business considerations into the platform of the widest public concern. Let us see what it means in other States besides Alabama. Statistics are scanty and difficult to obtain, but there are some established facts which are significant enough.

In Alabama the proportion of such young children to grown workers is between six and seven per cent., or between 500 and 600 in the twenty-four mills I visited. In Augusta, Ga., a count was made in June, 1900, through eight mills, and 556 children under twelve were found working. In South Carolina Mr. John B. Cleveland, president of the Whitney mills, giving evidence before the legislature, stated that thirty per cent. of the operatives in the Whitney mills were under twelve, and Mr. James L. Orr, president of the Piedmont mills, South Carolina, that twenty-five per cent. of his machinery was run by such children. The statement sometimes made that the number of children affected is so small that it is not worth public attention is not borne out by these figures, nor by the fact that in Georgia as many as thirty mill presidents appeared before the legislature to defeat the child-labor bill there.

It is important to notice that it is not only the cotton operatives who are affected by child-labor. During the recent agitation in England, which led to the age of the half timers in the cotton mills being raised from eleven to twelve, it was found both in Yorkshire and Lancashire that less than two-thirds of these were the children of workers in the mills. On the face of it no working population can have thirty per cent. between the ages of eight and twelve; so the presumption is that in mills where this is the percentage under twelve among the operatives, workpeople of other trades are sending their children into the mills to supplement their own earnings. I found this supposition confirmed by letters printed in the report of Mr. Lacy,[1] the commissioner of labor, in North Carolina. In several, sentences like these occur: "I am not in the mill myself, but represent it with my children;" "I am a carpenter, but have had children in the mill."

In time, therefore, the earning, and with the earning the spending capacity of workers in other trades will be lessened, and the development of local trade be checked, even though the cotton mills may make large dividends.

Another disastrous tendency of unregulated child-labor is to substitute the woman and the child for the man. In North Carolina some of the mill-owners speak complacently of their operatives being "loyal and peaceable, because composed chiefly of women and children." Many managers expressed the hope to me that they might soon be able to do without men almost entirely.

Prophecy about the cotton trade requires a map of the world. On the west coast of Africa, by the French, German, and English, in Egypt by the English, cotton is being grown with as good a staple for manufacturing purposes as that of the Southern States. Cotton factories will rise in these places before long, with unlimited "cheap" labor, albeit unintelligent and incapable of any great development, and it will be possible to manufacture coarse grades of yarn and cloth at incredibly low cost. The ground of competition for the Southern States will then be shifted to the fine grades,

[1] Benjamin R. Lacy.

which require intelligent, educated operatives, and the palm will fall to the place having the most technically educated workers. Chances for success seem small in the face of the largely illiterate cotton operatives of the Southern States. The waste and degeneration of these workers are the rankest folly. They are a splendid stock, in parts at least Scotch-Irish, spoiled somewhat by their isolation and the hard lives they have led, but capable of any development — more indeed than many of the foreign emigrant workers of the North. The one great advantage the North possesses over the South at the present moment lies in the education of the workers and the possibility of their physical development. How can the cotton operatives of the South keep their vitality when even the physical development permitted to the Negro children in the days of slavery is denied to the children of the poor whites? In England it has been proved that 4 to 6 hours a day in the mills for the children of factory operatives between the ages of 11 and 13 stunts their growth to the extent of 6 inches, and diminishes their weight by 22 pounds below the average English child, who is a full day scholar up to 13. What then must be the effect of 12 hours a day in a warmer climate on the children of a people unused to labor indoors?

Turning back once more to the purely human aspect of this uncivilized system, I would say that no array of facts and figures are needed by those who have seen it in operation. I am familiar with the slums of two continents, but I can say I have never seen a more pitiful sight than the mill children, nor known little ones for whom the outlook was more hopeless. It is not only that they are pale, shrunken and bowed — they look as if their brains were hypnotized and their souls paralyzed. A friend of mine in Atlanta, thinking to give some of these little victims a treat, asked a number out to her place in the country and turned them into the woods to play. What was her distress and amazement to find that they did not know what the word or the thing meant. Children in America who do not know how to play! And dividends from these mills are used probably for philanthropy, temperance, and missions! I even heard of one mill Sunday school where the children were told that God had put it into the hearts of good men to open a cotton mill that they might earn money so as to be able to put a nickel into the missionary box!

The plea urged that the operatives desire no change seems to me especially cowardly. Knowing nothing of economics they imagine themselves deprived not only of their children's earnings, but of their own by any restrictive law. In every place where the operatives are intelligent and independent enough to form any combination their feeling is largely in favor of legal restriction of child-labor. This is so in North Carolina, South

Carolina, and beginning to be so in Georgia. The only possible thing to be done is for public pressure to be brought to bear on the Legislatures of the Southern States to pass a law with at least the following provisions:

No child under twelve to be admitted into the factory, unless a widowed mother or invalided father should be totally dependent on that child for support, and in no case for a child to be admitted under ten.

Night work forbidden and hours limited to sixty a week for children under sixteen.

A slight educational test required and three months a year in school up to fourteen provided for.

Northern and Southern capitalists should be warned by their work-people in the North and their fellow-citizens to withdraw their opposition to the passage of such a law.

The opposition at present is immense. When I returned from my tour of investigation in Alabama I found the whole community, except those directly interested financially in cotton mills, on my side. The press, the pulpit, the schools, the women in their various clubs, took the matter up. A bill was presented at the second session of the Alabama Legislature, in the upper and lower houses, by gentlemen who had no connection with the labor movement.

The mill-owners immediately engaged two able lawyers, who were also professional lobbyists, to deal with the members of the Legislature on the subject. Representatives were warned that the local bills they had been sent up to pass would have small prospect of success should they vote for a child-labor law. At the hearing before the joint committees of the House and Senate the Senate Chamber was packed to overflowing. The mill-owners' interest was represented by a lawyer, who was also the president of a cotton mill, the owners of which are "philanthropic" Northern people — a corporation clergyman and a railway attorney. None of these men ever touched on the pros and cons of child-labor. The sincerity of their arguments may be gauged by their bringing forward a miserable little petition against the bill, written on the official paper of a very small mill, and signed by seventeen of its operatives.

The hearing was simply a public bluff. It appeared that the rejection of the bill had been settled beforehand in spite of public excitement upon the question. Similar defeats were recently experienced in Georgia and South Carolina, where the educated women have been making gallant efforts to get the need for child-labor legislation recognized. It is evident that only concerted and organized action through all the Southern States would be of any use on the part of all those interested in the question. Arrangements have accordingly been made to have the subject thoroughly ventilated and an agitation carried on for the introduction of a practically uniform bill into all the Southern Legislatures. A child-labor bill passed the Tennessee Legislature in the spring of this year, and has probably sounded the first stroke of the death knell of this abominable system. I cannot help hoping, though it seems visionary, that this is what the fight against child-labor may do in the South. The discussion of the subject reveals how closely the interests of all classes are united and the danger and futility of permitting the exploitation of the weakest.

What shall it profit the South if stockholders, North or South, gain the whole dividend and these States lose their children? "There is no wealth but life."

ALEXANDER J. McKELWAY

Child Labor in the Southern Cotton Mills

1906

The son of a Presbyterian minister, Alexander J. McKelway (1866–1918) was born in Pennsylvania but grew up in Virginia and graduated from Presbyterian Hampden-Sydney College and Union Theological Seminary, then located near Farmville, Virginia. Holding pastorates in North Carolina, McKelway became active in home mission work and, eventually, in the Prohibition movement in Fayetteville, where he served as pastor of the First Presbyterian Church. In 1898 he became editor of the statewide Presbyterian newspaper, the North Carolina Presbyterian, *and subsequently he became actively involved in other social reforms of the Progressive Era. Of particular interest to McKelway was the issue of child labor. As a Presbyterian editor and, after 1903, as editor of the* Charlotte News, *he wrote editorials opposing the use of child labor in textile mills.*

McKelway was perhaps best known as southern secretary of the National Child Labor Committee. Assuming the post in 1904, McKelway traveled the South promoting legislation limiting the use of children in mills.

This document is one of many addresses that McKelway gave explaining the need for reform.

Alexander J. McKelway, "Child Labor in the Southern Cotton Mills," *Annals of the American Academy of Political and Social Science* 27 (Jan.–June 1906): 259–69.

One day last week the train from Memphis, Tennessee, to Spartanburg, South Carolina, through the far famed Land of the Sky, carried a company of fifty people bound for the South Carolina cotton mills. Among those on board who expressed themselves on the subject of these emigrants from Tennessee, were the agent in charge of the emigrants, the conductor of the train, a business man from West Tennessee, a missionary school teacher, a minister of the gospel; while a secretary of the Child Labor Committee[1] took notes of what was said and reserved expression of opinion until now. It might be said that the business and professional life of the South was fairly well represented.

The minister happened to be a valued member of our North Carolina Child Labor Committee, and, of course, deplored the breaking up of these mountain homes, be they ever so humble, and recognized that the Church had little chance to influence the child when the mill had once claimed him. The school teacher, who had given her life with self-sacrificing zeal to educating the children of the mountaineers, felt that the child was equally beyond the reach of the school when the mill had made the demand for his labor. She was intimately acquainted with the life of the people, knew the bitterness of their poverty in some instances, but she felt that it was nothing short of a calamity for the children to be removed from their mountain farms to the cotton mills. The business man declaimed in two languages, English and the profane, against the scarcity of labor on the farms of West Tennessee on account of this steady draining of the tenant population from the farms to the mills, and he felt the unfair competition that came from the employment of children at man's work and woman's work in the mill, of course the business of the towns suffering from the non-productivity of the farms, through the scarcity of labor. But the conductor of the train was the most vehement in his denunciation of the mills themselves for the employment of children. He had seen these people leaving their native hills in the full tide of vigorous manhood and womanhood, with rosy-cheeked children. And he had seen some of them return, broken in health and spirits, the fair pictures that had been painted for them by the agent blotted out in the tears of disappointment. If he had thought of the economic view of the question as concerning his own occupation, he would have known that the children who went into the cotton mills in tender years would never be fit in manhood for work on the railroad, with its demand for intelligent and alert workmen. But the point is that the people of the South are talking about this evil of child labor in the cotton mills, and that public sentiment

[1] That is, the National Child Labor Committee.

is turning against the industry itself, with indiscriminate condemnation for the permission of such a system.

The agent of the cotton mills was the only one who regarded his work of inducing these people to leave their homes as a benefaction and himself as the advance agent of civilization. He said that he had found the worst conditions on the Pigeon River, in East Tennessee, among the Great Smoky Mountains. He had found fifteen living in one hut, who were glad enough to leave it for the mills; that there was no work for the women and children to do except in corn-planting or potato-digging time, while all could work in the mill, wet weather or dry, hot or cold; that he had thirty-two people on board for whom he had to pay half or full fare, besides the children; that he had made seven "shipments" from Newport, Tenn., averaging fifteen to the shipment; that seven more shipments had gone from Cleveland; that he must have shipped five hundred emigrants in all; that he represented an immigration association which had other agents out beside himself, and here he showed me one of the contracts to be signed by the emigrant, representing the cotton mill community as a sort of earthly paradise, with its free schools, free libraries, amusement halls, and secret order rooms, indicating that the twelve-hour day of the cotton mills left considerable time for leisure and culture; that the family was a great deal better off in the mill, where the whole family could make $3.75 a day, than on the farm, where the father had been able to make but seventy-five cents a day; that the law did not allow a child under twelve to work unless it was a "widder lady's" child, who is worked as young as he is able to work — presumably as the penalty for partial orphanage; that the parent was supposed to know how old his child was, and his word was taken as to the child's age, though, of course, there were a-plenty of children of six and eight and ten years in the mills, because their parents lied about their ages.

And then we undertook a little personal investigation of the children themselves. Little Harrison Swan was "going on ten" and was going to work in the Four Mills, at Greenville, S.C., and I doubt not is at work there now. Charley Matthews and a little comrade of about his size were each "about nine," and both were bound for the mills. And it made one's heart bleed to see the number of children younger still, and the babies at the breast, soon to be cast into the brazen arms of our modern Moloch.[2] For, as our chairman said in an address last year, these people are of the purest American stock on this continent. North Carolina has a law requiring a cotton mill agent to take out a license that costs him a hundred dollars. And yet, from the little village of Clyde, on the Western North Carolina

---

[2] Moloch, Semitic god in the ancient world, was worshiped through the sacrifice of children.

Railway, there went last year to the South Carolina cotton mills fifteen hundred men, women and children of this pure Anglo-Saxon stock, whose fathers fought at King's Mountain and New Orleans against the British,[3] who fought on both sides in the Civil War, for the right as it was given each to see the right; who were the first to volunteer in the war with Spain, but to whom the nation will turn in the hour of her need in vain, as England looked to Manchester and Leeds and Sheffield in vain for men to conquer a handful of South African farmers,[4] when the strength and vigor of her soldiers had been sapped by premature and long continued labor in the mills.

So it is that Tennessee, which has but thirty cotton mills of her own, is affected by the cotton mill industry of South Carolina which stands next to Massachusetts in the number of spindles. The problem of child labor is one that affects the South as a whole and touches it at a point which it has hitherto most jealously guarded, the preservation of the vigor of its Anglo-Saxon stock. Nay, we make bold to say that child labor in the South is more a national question than child labor in New England or Pennsylvania. For in the North and East it is chiefly the children of the foreigners that need protection. No child of American stock has been found in the sweatshops of New York City. But in the South, it is the breed of American that is threatened with degeneration.

To those unacquainted with actual conditions, the subject assigned me might be supposed to have an unjustly discriminating title. Why consider the cotton mills as the only industry cursed with child labor? It is true that there are several hundred thousand children of the South reported in the census as engaged in "gainful occupations." But the large majority of these are at work on the farms, under the eye of their parents, and would not be counted ordinarily except for the peculiarities of the tenant system in the South. This work is not only harmless, but helpful, save where it interferes with attendance at school. It is true also that there are some very young children employed in the tobacco factories of Virginia and North Carolina, in the cigar factories of Florida, in the woolen mills of Kentucky and Tennessee, in the coal mines of West Virginia and Alabama. But the evil here is slight in comparison with the child slavery of the cotton mills. . . .

---

[3] The Battle of King's Mountain was fought during the American Revolution, on October 7, 1780, just south of the North Carolina–South Carolina border southwest of Charlotte, N.C. It resulted in victory for the Patriot side. The Battle of New Orleans was fought on January 8, 1815, during the War of 1812, and resulted in a major American defeat of the British attackers.
[4] The reference here is to the Boer War (1899–1902), which was fought between British forces and the descendants of Dutch settlers in South Africa, who are known as Boers.

This industry is centered in the four cotton producing states of the South, Alabama, Georgia, and the two Carolinas. These mills are mainly located in the Piedmont section of these four states. Alabama has sixty-five cotton manufacturing establishments of all kinds, Georgia 169, South Carolina 163, and North Carolina 315. But these figures from the last Blue Book are probably already antiquated. The South still sends to foreign countries 65 per cent. of the cotton she produces. But it is now manufacturing into yarn and cloth a little more than half of the remaining 35 per cent. It would seem only a question of time when the cotton mill in the cotton field, other conditions being equal, must successfully compete with the cotton mill in Philadelphia or New England, the two other cotton manufacturing centers of the United States, and with the cotton mills of Old England as well. It is estimated that within sixty miles of Charlotte, N.C., there is enough water power to drive two-thirds of the spindles of England; that is, a million horse-power. In Alabama it is possible from a cotton factory to fire a rifle bullet into a coal mine and then throw a stone into a cotton field. The New England companies that own mills in both New England and the South find their dividends twice or thrice as great from their Southern mills. And it may be added here that they are conspicuous opponents of any legislation in the South that would diminish the labor of children, and that their representatives throng the halls of legislation for the repeal of such inadequate laws as we have and for the blocking of all humane legislation.

It is difficult for any one not reared in the South to understand the interest and pride that this expansion of the cotton mill industry has caused among us. The farmer has attributed to this increase of spindles and to the local demand for spot cotton the advance in the price of the staple that is at the foundation of Southern prosperity. The railroads are dependent in large measure for the increase in tonnage upon the output of the cotton mills, and there has been in several states a hard and fast alliance between the railroads and the cotton mills in opposition to any legislation directed against child labor. It may, perhaps, not be out of place to mention the obvious fact that successful competition with New England in its chosen field of manufacture has added some zest and spice to the building up of this industry and to the favor with which the people have hitherto regarded it.

There are now employed in Southern cotton mills, according to the "Blue Book" of 1904–5, which is already a year old, 238,881 operatives. Counting the new mills that have gone into operation since, there must be a quarter of a million people thus employed. Of these, a former president of the Cotton Manufacturers' Association estimates that only

30 per cent. are adults, though by adults he means those over twenty-one. The president of the American Cotton Manufacturing Association, Mr. R. M. Miller, of Charlotte, N.C., in an interview deprecating the raising of the age limit in North Carolina from twelve to fourteen for girls and for illiterate boys, claimed that 75 per cent. of the spinners of North Carolina were fourteen or under. The average for children under sixteen employed in Southern mills, as given by the census of 1900, was 25 per cent. On that basis there must be 60,000 children, from six to sixteen, now working in the mills of the Southern States, and my own opinion is that there are 60,000 under fourteen years of age. And just now the mills are running night and day, and even the rule of sixty-six hours a week makes the working day for these little ones for five days of the week twelve hours.

But while there are natural advantages for the manufacture of cotton near the fields where it is produced, it is a fact easily proved that the child labor system of the South is an advantage to Northern mills. The employment of children is an economic error in that it tends to lower the standard of efficiency in industry and to use up the labor supply in exactly the same way that the putting of colts to the plough would do in agricultural communities. In the Georgia Legislature last summer a noted cotton manufacturer, a member of the Georgia Senate, in an eloquent plea against the child labor system, challenged his associates in that business who were also members of the Senate, to disprove his statement: that the same quality of cotton goods manufactured in the South was sold at a price from two to four cents a pound lower than these goods manufactured in the North. The New England mills that are prospering the most have thrown their old machinery upon the scrap pile and have ceased competition with the South by manufacturing the finer goods, in which there is the greater margin of profit. Mills for the manufacture of these finer goods are now being erected in the South, but the demand goes up from them for a better class of labor, and it is another economic truth that the child laborer does not ordinarily develop into a skilled laborer. A Georgia cotton mill imported skilled laborers for the manufacture of fine goods. The goods were sold at Philadelphia and New England prices. Once some tags containing the name and location of this mill were slipped into the bales of finished cloth by the workmen. The mill management immediately received a letter from the commission merchant urging that this should never be done again; that he had concealed the fact that this particular mill was located in the South, and thereby had been able to get Northern prices for the goods. What a short-sighted policy it is, for the profit of the moment, to be wasting the opportunity for building up at the South an industry that shall be distinguished from the same industry in both New England and Old England, by being free at once from the long hours and the low wages and the infant labor that have been the curse of the cotton mill for a hundred years, and are chiefly now the curse of the Southern cotton mills.

And, as was shown in the introduction to this address, the people of the South are beginning to feel that the present methods of this industry are exacting too great a price for its prosperity. Physicians, individually and in their state conventions, are . . . protesting against the depreciation of the human stock by this cruel system; against the very presence in a cotton mill, with its flying lint, of young children with their more delicate lungs; are pointing out the frequent cases of throat and lung diseases they are treating in their hospitals among their little patients from the mills; and especially are protesting against the physical injury to young girls, at the critical period of their lives, and the necessary injury to the future race that is involved. The farmer is beginning to protest against the unfair competition between the mill and the farm in the labor market, the tenant being persuaded to leave the farm for the factory by the inducement that he can put his young children to work at profitable wages, reversing both the law of nature and the law of Scripture, that the parent should lay up for the child and not the child for the parent. The educational leaders are making bitter protest against the increase of illiteracy in the factory districts, and we do not need any increase of illiteracy in the South. The Southern pulpit, with united voice, is crying aloud and sparing not, inveighing against man's inhumanity to children. The politician is beginning to feel this wave of public indignation against the evil. The Southern press, religious and secular, great dailies and country weeklies, with the exception of the mercenary few, are pointing out the inevitable tendency of child labor in the mills, the fact that the very supremacy of the white race is involved, since the negro is not employed in the cotton mills and his children are freed from that slavery. Southern patriots everywhere are proclaiming that the child should be put above the dividend, that the place for the child is not the mill, but the school. Even the stockholders of the mills are beginning to feel that their profits are of the nature of blood-money and are too dearly won at the price of the lives and the health of the little children. And there are many humane mill owners who, despite the feeling that they should stand together against restrictive legislation, in spite of the false fear that the child labor opponents are labor agitators, are unwilling to play the role of the infamous Herods[5] who "sought the young child's life." In the three States of North Carolina, South Carolina, and Alabama, where a twelve-year limit has been established by law, many are trying honestly to observe that law, even with no provision of law enforcement and no system

[5] The reference here is to Herod the Great (73–4 B.C.), who, fearing the prophecy about a coming Messiah, ordered the murder of all infants in Jerusalem.

of factory inspection or even of birth registration; and I am persuaded that in Georgia, unique among the manufacturing States of Europe or America in having no child labor law, many manufacturers, because they are honorable men, resent the reproach that has been brought upon them as a class by the wholesale violation of their own agreement not to employ young children, which is a matter of common knowledge. One of them proclaimed in the Georgia Legislature that the reason he had refused to join the Georgia Industrial Association was that he was unwilling to contribute, as a member of the association, to a legislative fund for preventing a child labor law. In spite of the ineffectiveness of present laws and the violation of solemn agreements and the utter absence of protective legislation in some of the states, I make bold to say, because I know my people and love my people, that the South is too kind-hearted to allow this sacrifice of the children. They know that "to be a man too soon is to be a small man." They believe, with John Ruskin,[6] that "it is a shame for a nation to make its young girls weary." And it is a Southern state, Louisiana, that is unique in making a difference of two years in the age limit for employment between the boys and girls, and in favor of the girls.

The child is the saviour of the race. What we do for the child, for his protection, for his education, for his training for the duties of manhood, for securing the rights and prolonging the period of childhood, is the measure of what we shall accomplish for the race that is to be. The ancient Hebrew prophet drew a picture of the golden age of the world, that with the Hebrew and the Christian is still in the future, a picture that has never been surpassed in literature. And the central figure on the canvas is that of the little child. The sucking child shall play on the hole of the asp. And when the wolf shall dwell with the lamb, the leopard shall lie down with the kid, the lion shall eat straw like the ox, the cow and the bear shall feed — a little child shall lead them. And so it must be with this civilization of ours, if it is to endure.

Forces of leonine violence, forces of serpentine cunning, forces of wolfish greed, as well as the forces of peaceful industry and domestic labor, must consent to be led in peaceful procession, while walking before them, drawing their might with his innocence, and his helplessness and his promise, is the figure of the little child. God speed the day! God hasten the coming of the age when the child shall not be driven but shall lead, when the child shall not be the prey of the giant forces that are now contending for the mastery, but shall quell and tame their violence and inaugurate the reign of universal brotherhood.

[6] John Ruskin (1819–1900), English writer, critic, and artist.

LEWIS W. HINE

Photographic Essay:
Child Labor in the New South
1908–1911

Employing modern media, child-labor reformers effectively exposed the extent of working children through the use of photographs. A pioneer investigative photographer was the New York police reporter and journalist Jacob Riis (1849–1914), whose classic How the Other Half Lives *(1890) dramatized poverty in New York City tenement housing. In 1908, the National Child Labor Committee (NCLC) hired Wisconsin native Lewis W. Hine, who had already earned a reputation for his photographs of Ellis Island immigrants and for his photojournalistic investigation of social conditions in Pittsburgh. Working eleven years with the NCLC, Hine eventually traveled twelve thousand miles around the country photographing child workers in textile mills, canneries, and coal mines of New England, the South, and mid-Atlantic states.*

The following eight photographs offer examples of Hine's work between 1908 and 1911 in the mill communities of six cotton textile states in the South.

Figure 1. Girl tending textile machinery in a North Carolina textile mill, November 1908. The mill was located in Cherryville, a mill village in Gaston County, in the heart of the industrial belt of the Carolina Piedmont.
Figure 2. Small girl working at textile mill, December 1908. Located in Newberry, South Carolina, this girl was employed at Mollahan Mills.
Figure 3. Young children employed at Mollahan Mills in Newberry, South Carolina, December 1908.
Figure 4. Working children at King Mill, Augusta, Georgia, January 1909.
Figure 5. The entire labor force of Elk Cotton Mills in Fayetteville, Tennessee, November 1910. Young boy at extreme left was classified as a "helper," a young child accompanying his mother to work.
Figure 6. Two small children at work at Loudon Hosiery Mills, Loudon, Tennessee, December 1910.
Figure 7. Young spinner in Yazoo City, Mississippi, May 1911.
Figure 8. Part of the workforce at Washington Cotton Mills, Fries, Virginia, May 1911.

The photographs are from John R. Kemp, *Lewis Hine: Photographs of Child Labor in the New South* (Jackson and London: University Press of Mississippi, 1986). Reprinted by permission of the University Press.

Figure 1 ▲

Figure 2 ▼

Figure 3 ▲

Figure 4 ▼

Figure 5 ▲

Figure 6 ▼

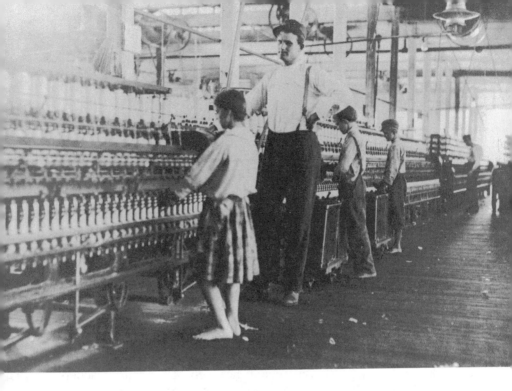

Figure 7 ▲

Figure 8 ▼

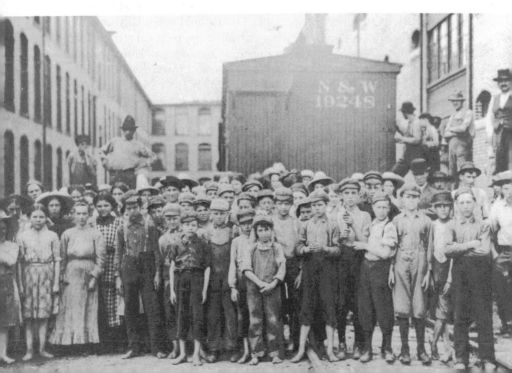

5

Black Education

Southern social reformers focused on schools as a particularly crucial element in their efforts to regenerate the South. In 1901, the crusade to reform southern schools began with the organization of the Southern Education Board (SEB) and, a year later, of the General Education Board (GEB) (which received a large bequest from John D. Rockefeller). Both the SEB and GEB coordinated far-reaching campaigns seeking to convert public opinion to a greater commitment to public education. The results of their efforts were considerable. Southern state legislatures sharply increased appropriations for education from the dismally low nineteenth-century levels; school officials promoted local efforts to modernize southern public education by constructing new schools, training teachers, revamping the curriculum, and expanding the length of the school year.

Yet virtually all of these efforts, at least before about 1910, benefited only whites. Many school reformers believed that changing white schools first would lead to wider consequences that would eventually help black schools. Because southern whites controlled the political structure and southern blacks lacked the vote, public funding for school modernization and improvement soon became grossly skewed toward white schools. The first consolidated rural schools — in which one-room schools were replaced by large, multiroom, permanent structures — were always white. White teachers' salaries rose steadily during the Progressive Era, whereas black teachers' salaries stagnated. And efforts to lengthen the extent and reach of schools, by expanding school terms and increasing efforts to compel attendance, largely bypassed black schools. As Booker T. Washington sadly concluded in 1910, white school reform had occurred at the "expense of Negro education" and had effectively taken from black schools in order to "advance the education of white people."[1] In summary, school reform — in more obvious ways than other varieties of reform — exposed a fatal flaw in southern Progressivism.

---

[1] Booker T. Washington to James Hardy Dillard, July 30, 1909, in Louis R. Harlan et al., eds., *The Booker T. Washington Papers,* 13 vols. (Urbana: University of Illinois Press, 1972–1984), 10:153.

Despite an unequal system of schools, African Americans enthusiastically supported education. During and after the Civil War, northern white missionaries established the first schools for freed people; interdenominational organizations such as the American Missionary Association maintained these schools and founded the first black colleges. The Freedman's Bureau, which began during the closing months of the Civil War in 1865, also supported efforts at African American education. By the 1870s, the South — as a part of the price that Congress imposed for readmission to the Union — had established a public education system composed of segregated schools for whites and blacks.

By 1900, a generation of African Americans had experienced public education. Although most blacks agreed on the significance of education to their progress, there were sharp philosophical disagreements, exemplified best by the debate between William E. Burghardt Du Bois and Booker T. Washington. Their debate was, in many ways, a clash of styles and approaches, but their messages of militancy or accommodation, assimilation or separation, were fundamental issues. Washington's "industrial" approach to black education was well known by the turn of the twentieth century. It had been most widely publicized at Hampton Institute in Virginia, which Washington attended in the 1870s, and at Tuskegee Institute in Alabama, which Washington founded in 1881. At Hampton and Tuskegee, the industrial education approach rejected the traditional classical curriculum and embraced a back-to-basics approach to schooling. African Americans in industrial schools learned values of thrift, sobriety, and hard work. In Washington's view (see p. 120), African Americans needed first to obtain economic autonomy and independence before striving for political power. Du Bois saw the matter differently (see p. 114). Rather than a bootstraps approach, Du Bois endorsed the development of a black elite capable of challenging racial inequity and oppression; he focused on the "talented tenth" of black Americans.

Reform-minded whites were also engaged in the debate about black education. In the context of a separate-and-unequal segregated school system, they were aware of the widening disparities between white and black schools. Many of them also realized that any vision of the progress and development of the South out of underdevelopment and poverty depended on at least a degree of black progress. Virtually all of these white reformers favored segregated schools, to be sure, and the reforms that they envisioned focused for the most part on the Hampton-Tuskegee version of industrial education. This meant physical improvements over the dilapidated black schools across the rural South, but it also meant introducing an industrial curriculum that emphasized moral attitudes toward work and basic skills rather than the study of abstract academic subjects such as Greek and Latin, English, philosophy, or history.

Northern philanthropy played an especially key role in efforts to reform black education. The General Education Board took an early interest, as one of its field agents, Leo M. Favrot of Louisiana, suggests in the third document in this chapter (see p. 125). By the time of the outbreak of World War I, the GEB had been sponsoring, in conjunction with another northern philanthropy, the Slater Fund, the teaching of black teachers along industrial lines at county training schools. These county training schools, which the GEB operated and supported along with southern state educational officials, became early versions of public black high schools across the rural South. Along with the GEB, other northern philanthropies became active in black education after 1910. In 1904, the Philadelphia Quaker philanthropist Anna T. Jeanes gave Booker T. Washington and Hollis B. Frissell, principal of Hampton Institute, $10,000 each to stimulate the improvement of rural black elementary schools; a year later, she donated $200,000 to the GEB to initiate a campaign on a larger scale. Then, in 1907, Jeanes added $1 million to be used for the "rudimentary education" of southern rural blacks.[2]

In 1908, the Jeanes Fund began an ambitious program to infuse industrial education among rural African Americans. In that year, Virginia Estelle Randolph, a black teacher in Henrico County, Virginia, became the first "Jeanes teacher" — an African American who visited rural communities and sought to improve black schools and to institute an industrial curriculum. By 1920, there were 272 Jeanes teachers in the South, and they became missionaries of black educational reform.

Other efforts to change black education also appeared at about the same time. In 1912, Julius Rosenwald, a partner in the department store Sears, Roebuck, and Company, donated money to Tuskegee to finance industrial education in Alabama. Within three years, by 1915, Rosenwald was persuaded to finance a wide-ranging Rosenwald Fund, and over the next decade it helped to finance, in partnership with state financial support, the construction of some 5,357 new rural black schools in fifteen states in southern and border states. Northern philanthropies such as the GEB, Jeanes Fund, and Rosenwald Fund were careful to work with southern school officials, and soon their efforts gained a general coordination

---

[2] On the origins of the Jeanes Fund, see Lance George Edward Jones, *The Jeanes Teacher in the United States, 1908–1933: An Account of Twenty-Five Years' Experience in the Supervision of Negro Rural Schools* (Chapel Hill: University of North Carolina Press, 1933).

through the establishment of school agents for black schools. The first such official was Jackson Davis, appointed in 1910 as the supervisor of Negro schools for Virginia; within a year, six other southern states had followed suit. These state supervisors served as coordinators of various philanthropic and state efforts to improve black education, and they visited and reported on the conditions of black schools. They directed the Jeanes efforts at teacher training and the GEB program of county training schools, and, eventually, helped to oversee the Rosenwald school building program. Most important, perhaps, these supervisors served as liaisons among state educational officials, northern philanthropists, and local African American communities.

Serious obstacles preventing modernization in black education remained. Disfranchisement eliminated African Americans as a political constituency in the South, and southern whites in power were not accountable to them for disparities in the segregated school system. Those disparities continued throughout the first half of the twentieth century, as the documents in this chapter clearly indicate. Perhaps the clearest evidence of the widening gap between white and black schools appeared in high school education. Mass high school education in the South, before the 1920s, meant white high schools. To cite the example of one state, all but three of Virginia's one hundred counties had high schools in 1920, but only sixteen had black high schools. Even more striking, although 22,061 white students in rural Virginia attended high schools in 1920, only 297 black pupils did so.[3]

Black education offers important insights into the objectives of southern Progressivism — and some of its major tensions. When reading the documents in this chapter, consider the following questions:

1. What important principles are involved in the debate between Du Bois and Washington? To whom does each author appeal?
2. How does the white reformer in this chapter, Favrot, view black education? What does he believe are its main deficiencies? What does he see as the main causes and solutions of its deficiencies?
3. How do black reformers such as Washington differ from white reformers such as Favrot? What are their most important assumptions and goals, and how do they differ?
4. What does "industrial" education mean to each author of the documents in this chapter?

[3] William A. Link, *A Hard Country and a Lonely Place: Schooling, Society, and Reform in Rural Virginia, 1870–1920* (Chapel Hill: University of North Carolina Press, 1986), 189.

W. E. B. DU BOIS

Of the Training of Black Men

1903

Born in Massachusetts, William Edward Burghardt Du Bois (1868–1963) received a scholarship to attend Fisk University, in Nashville, Tennessee, from which he graduated in 1888. He then attended Harvard College, receiving a B.A. degree in 1890 and, five years later, a Ph.D. degree — the first African American to obtain a doctorate at Harvard. Du Bois's subsequent career as sociologist, historian, social critic, editor, poet, activist, and reformer displayed a brilliant and wide-ranging mind. A founder of the National Association for the Advancement of Colored People (NAACP), Du Bois served as longtime editor of that organization's chief mouthpiece, The Crisis.

In 1903, Du Bois was propelled to worldwide fame with the publication of The Souls of Black Folk, *from which this document is taken. Here and elsewhere in* Souls, *Du Bois opposes the educational and reform program of Booker T. Washington.*

. . . In rough approximation we may point out four varying decades of work in Southern education since the Civil War. From the close of the war until 1876, was the period of uncertain groping and temporary relief. There were army schools, mission schools, and schools of the Freedman's Bureau in chaotic disarrangement seeking system and coöperation. Then followed ten years of constructive definite effort toward the building of complete school systems in the South. Normal schools[1] and colleges were founded for the freedmen, and teachers trained there to man the public schools. There was the inevitable tendency of war to underestimate the prejudices of the master and the ignorance of the slave, and all seemed clear sailing out of the wreckage of the storm. Meantime, starting in this decade yet especially developing from 1885 to 1895, began the industrial revolution of the South. The land saw glimpses of a new destiny and the stirring of new ideals. The educational system striving to

[1] Teacher training institutions.

William Edward Burghardt Du Bois, *The Souls of Black Folk: Essays and Sketches* (1903; reprint, edited with an introduction by Nathan Hare and Alvin F. Poussaint, New York and Scarborough, Ontario: New American Library, 1982).

complete itself saw new obstacles and a field of work ever broader and deeper. The Negro colleges, hurriedly founded, were inadequately equipped, illogically distributed, and of varying efficiency and grade; the normal and high schools were doing little more than common-school work, and the common schools[2] were training but a third of the children who ought to be in them, and training these too often poorly. At the same time the white South, by reason of its sudden conversion from the slavery ideal, by so much the more became set and strengthened in its racial prejudice, and crystallized it into harsh law and harsher custom; while the marvellous pushing forward of the poor white daily threatened to take even bread and butter from the mouths of the heavily handicapped sons of the freedmen. In the midst, then, of the larger problem of Negro education sprang up the more practical question of work, the inevitable economic quandary that faces a people in the transition from slavery to freedom, and especially those who make that change amid hate and prejudice, lawlessness and ruthless competition.

The industrial school springing to notice in this decade, but coming to full recognition in the decade beginning with 1895, was the proffered answer to this combined educational and economic crisis, and an answer of singular wisdom and timeliness. . . .

When turning our eyes from the temporary and the contingent in the Negro problem to the broader question of the permanent uplifting and civilization of black men in America, we have a right to inquire, as this enthusiasm for material advancement mounts to its height, if after all the industrial school is the final and sufficient answer in the training of the Negro race; and to ask gently, but in all sincerity, the ever-recurring query of the ages, Is not life more than meat, and the body more than raiment? And men ask this to-day all the more eagerly because of sinister signs in recent educational movements. The tendency is here, born of slavery and quickened to renewed life by the crazy imperialism of the day, to regard human beings as among the material resources of a land to be trained with an eye single to future dividends. Race-prejudices, which keep brown and black men in their "places," we are coming to regard as useful allies with such a theory, no matter how much they may dull the ambition and sicken the hearts of struggling human beings. And above all, we daily hear that an education that encourages aspiration, that sets the loftiest of ideals and seeks as an end culture and character rather than bread-winning, is the privilege of white men and the danger and delusion of black.

---

[2] "Common" schools, first established in New England in the early nineteenth century, were public schools that usually went no farther than the elementary grades.

Especially has criticism been directed against the former educational efforts to aid the Negro. In the four periods I have mentioned, we find first, boundless, planless enthusiasm and sacrifice; then the preparation of teachers for a vast public-school system; then the launching and expansion of that school system amid increasing difficulties; and finally the training of workmen for the new and growing industries. This development has been sharply ridiculed as a logical anomaly and flat reversal of nature. Soothly we have been told that first industrial and manual training should have taught the Negro to work, then simple schools should have taught him to read and write, and finally, after years, high and normal schools could have completed the system, as intelligence and wealth demanded.

That a system logically so complete was historically impossible, it needs but a little thought to prove. Progress in human affairs is more often a pull than a push, a surging forward of the exceptional man, and the lifting of his duller brethren slowly and painfully to his vantage-ground. Thus it was no accident that gave birth to universities centuries before the common schools, that made fair Harvard the first flower of our wilderness. So in the South: the mass of the freedmen at the end of the war lacked the intelligence so necessary to modern workingmen. They must first have the common school to teach them to read, write, and cipher; and they must have higher schools to teach teachers for the common schools. The white teachers who flocked South went to establish such a common-school system. Few held the idea of founding colleges; most of them at first would have laughed at the idea. But they faced, as all men since them have faced, that central paradox of the South, — the social separation of the races. At that time it was the sudden volcanic rupture of nearly all relations between black and white, in work and government and family life. Since then a new adjustment of relations in economic and political affairs has grown up, — an adjustment subtle and difficult to grasp, yet singularly ingenious, which leaves still that frightful chasm at the color-line across which men pass at their peril. Thus, then and now, there stand in the South two separate worlds; and separate not simply in the higher realms of social intercourse, but also in church and school, on railway and street-car, in hotels and theatres, in streets and city sections, in books and newspapers, in asylums and jails, in hospitals and graveyards. There is still enough of contact for large economic and group coöperation, but the separation is so thorough and deep that it absolutely precludes for the present between the races anything like that sympathetic and effective group-training and leadership of the one by the other, such as the American Negro and all backward peoples must have for effectual progress.

This the missionaries of '68 soon saw; and if effective industrial and trade schools were impracticable before the establishment of a common-school system, just as certainly no adequate common schools could be founded until there were teachers to teach them. Southern whites would not teach them; Northern whites in sufficient numbers could not be had. If the Negro was to learn, he must teach himself, and the most effective help that could be given him was the establishment of schools to train Negro teachers. This conclusion was slowly but surely reached by every student of the situation until simultaneously, in widely separated regions, without consultation or systematic plan, there arose a series of institutions designed to furnish teachers for the untaught. Above the sneers of critics at the obvious defects of this procedure must ever stand its one crushing rejoinder: in a single generation they put thirty thousand black teachers in the South; they wiped out the illiteracy of the majority of the black people of the land, and they made Tuskegee possible.

Such higher training-schools tended naturally to deepen broader development: at first they were common and grammar schools, then some became high schools. And finally, by 1900, some thirty-four had one year or more of studies of college grade. This development was reached with different degrees of speed in different institutions: Hampton is still a high school, while Fisk University started her college in 1871, and Spelman Seminary about 1896.[3] In all cases the aim was identical, — to maintain the standards of the lower training by giving teachers and leaders the best practicable training; and above all, to furnish the black world with adequate standards of human culture and lofty ideals of life. It was not enough that the teachers of teachers should be trained in technical normal methods; they must also, so far as possible, be broad-minded, cultured men and women, to scatter civilization among a people whose ignorance was not simply of letters, but of life itself.

It can thus be seen that the work of education in the South began with higher institutions of training, which threw off as their foliage common schools, and later industrial schools, and at the same time strove to shoot their roots ever deeper toward college and university training. . . .

Fifty years ago the ability of Negro students in any appreciable numbers to master a modern college course would have been difficult to prove. To-day it is proved by the fact that four hundred Negroes, many of whom have been reported as brilliant students, have received the bachelor's degree from Harvard, Yale, Oberlin, and seventy other leading

---

[3] Fisk University is located in Nashville, Tennessee; Spelman, in Atlanta.

colleges. Here we have, then, nearly twenty-five hundred Negro graduates, of whom the crucial query must be made, How far did their training
fit them for life? . . . Personally I know many hundreds of these graduates,
and have corresponded with more than a thousand; through others I have
followed carefully the life-work of scores; I have taught some of them and
some of the pupils whom they have taught, lived in homes which they
have builded, and looked at life through their eyes. Comparing them as
a class with my fellow students in New England and in Europe, I cannot
hesitate in saying that nowhere have I met men and women with a
broader spirit of helpfulness, with deeper devotion to their life-work, or
with more consecrated determination to succeed in the face of bitter
difficulties than among Negro college-bred men. . . .

Strange to relate! for this is certain, no secure civilization can be
built in the South with the Negro as an ignorant, turbulent proletariat.
Suppose we seek to remedy this by making them laborers and nothing
more: they are not fools, they have tasted of the Tree of Life, and they
will not cease to think, will not cease attempting to read the riddle of
the world. By taking away their best equipped teachers and leaders,
by slamming the door of opportunity in the faces of their bolder and
brighter minds, will you make them satisfied with their lot? or will you
not rather transfer their leading from the hands of men taught to think
to the hands of untrained demagogues? We ought not to forget that
despite the pressure of poverty, and despite the active discouragement
and even ridicule of friends, the demand for higher training steadily
increases among Negro youth: there were, in the years from 1875 to
1880, 22 Negro graduates from Northern colleges; from 1885 to 1890
there were 43, and from 1895 to 1900, nearly 100 graduates. From
Southern Negro colleges there were, in the same three periods, 143,413,
and over 500 graduates. Here, then, is the plain thirst for training; by
refusing to give this Talented Tenth the key to knowledge, can any
sane man imagine that they will lightly lay aside their yearning and
contentedly become hewers of wood and drawers of water?

No. The dangerously clear logic of the Negro's position will more and
more loudly assert itself in that day when increasing wealth and more
intricate social organization preclude the South from being, as it so
largely is, simply an armed camp for intimidating black folk. Such waste
of energy cannot be spared if the South is to catch up with civilization.
And as the black third of the land grows in thrift and skill, unless skilfully
guided in its larger philosophy, it must more and more brood over the
red past and the creeping, crooked present, until it grasps a gospel of
revolt and revenge and throws its new-found energies athwart the current

of advance. Even to-day the masses of the Negroes see all too clearly the anomalies of their position and the moral crookedness of yours. . . .

I insist that the question of the future is how best to keep these millions from brooding over the wrongs of the past and the difficulties of the present, so that all their energies may be bent toward a cheerful striving and coöperation with their white neighbors toward a larger, juster, and fuller future. That one wise method of doing this lies in the closer knitting of the Negro to the great industrial possibilities of the South is a great truth. And this the common schools and the manual training and trade schools are working to accomplish. But these alone are not enough. The foundations of knowledge in this race, as in others, must be sunk deep in the college and university if we would build a solid, permanent structure. Internal problems of social advance must inevitably come, — problems of work and wages, of families and homes, of morals and the true valuing of the things of life; and all these and other inevitable problems of civilization the Negro must meet and solve largely for himself, by reason of his isolation; and can there be any possible solution other than by study and thought and an appeal to the rich experience of the past? Is there not, with such a group and in such a crisis, infinitely more danger to be apprehended from half-trained minds and shallow thinking than from over-education and over-refinement? Surely we have wit enough to found a Negro college so manned and equipped as to steer successfully between the *dilettante* and the fool. We shall hardly induce black men to believe that if their stomachs be full, it matters little about their brains. They already dimly perceive that the paths of peace winding between honest toil and dignified manhood call for the guidance of skilled thinkers, the loving, reverent comradeship between the black lowly and the black men emancipated by training and culture.

The function of the Negro college, then, is clear: it must maintain the standards of popular education, it must seek the social regeneration of the Negro, and it must help in the solution of problems of race contact and coöperation. And finally, beyond all this, it must develop men. . . .

BOOKER T. WASHINGTON

Why I Made Tuskegee an Industrial School

1912

Born a slave in Franklin County, in southern Virginia, Booker T. Washington became probably the best-known African American leader of his time. He was also a living example of one person's determination to succeed — a story that he recounts in his autobiography, Up from Slavery *(1901). Educated at Hampton Institute, a school established to educate southern blacks and Native Americans, Washington became a protégé of Hampton's white principal, the northern missionary Samuel Chapman Armstrong. In 1881, Washington founded a school in Black Belt Alabama largely based on Hampton's example, and during the 1880s and 1890s he became known as a leading exponent of industrial education. At the Cotton States and International Exposition in Atlanta, in September 1895, Washington delivered what became known as his Atlanta Compromise speech. In it, he told southern blacks to "cast down your buckets where they are" and focus on economic advancement. At the same time, to southern white listeners, Washington suggested that racial harmony could be based on separation of the races. "In all things that are purely social," Washington declared, blacks and whites could be "as separate as the fingers, yet one as the hand in all things essential to mutual progress."*

During the early 1900s, Washington headed up what became known as the Tuskegee Machine, and he dispensed political offices that derived from Republican patronage and funneled northern philanthropic support. But the basis of Washington's power and influence remained the Tuskegee model of black educational uplift. In the South, industrial education was in vogue as a common ground for African Americans and their southern white counterparts. By 1912, when Booker T. Washington delivered this address, his program of industrial education had become the most popular form of black educational reform in the South.

Tuskegee Institute was started in a small way in the summer of 1881. At that time the negro had lost practically all political control in the South. As

Booker T. Washington, "Why I Made Tuskegee an Industrial School," *The Papers of Booker T. Washington,* ed. Louis R. Harlan et al. 14 (Urbana: University of Illinois Press, 1972–1989), 11: 470–75.

early as 1885 there were scarcely any members of my race in the National Congress or state legislatures, and long before this date they had ceased to hold state offices. This was true, notwithstanding the protests and fervent oratory of such strong race leaders as Frederick Douglass, B. K. Bruce, P. B. S. Pinchback, and John M. Langston, with a host of others.[1] When Frederick Douglass, the greatest man that the negro has produced, died in 1895, it is safe to say that the negro in the Southern States, with here and there a few exceptions, had practically no political control or political influence, except in sending delegates to national conventions, or in holding a few Federal positions by appointment.

It became evident to many thoughtful negroes that the members of the race could no longer look to political agitation and the opportunity of holding office as a means of gaining a reputation or winning success. In short they must look to something more tangible and substantial upon which to base their future. It was at this period in the negro's development, when the distance between the races was greatest and the spirit and ambition of the colored people most depressed, that the idea of industrial or business development was introduced and began to be made prominent.

It did not take the more level-headed members of the race long to see that while the negro in the South was surrounded by many difficulties, there was practically no line drawn and little discrimination in the world of commerce, banking, storekeeping, manufacturing, the skilled trades, and in agriculture; and in this lay his great opportunity. They understood that, while the whites might object to a negro's being postmaster, they would not object to his being president of a bank, and in the latter occupation they would give him assistance and encouragement. The colored people were quick to see that while the negro would not be invited to attend the white man's prayer meeting, he would be invited every time to attend the stockholders' meetings of a business concern in which he had an interest, and that he could buy property in practically any portion of the South where the white man could buy it.

The white citizens were all the more willing to encourage the negro in this economic or industrial development, because they saw that the prosperity of the negro meant also the prosperity of the white man. They

---

[1] Frederick Douglass (1817–1895) was born a slave in Maryland but later became an abolitionist, journalist, and prominent black leader. Blanche Kelso Bruce (1841–1898) was a teacher and planter who became, in 1874, the second African American elected to the U.S. Senate. P. B. S. Pinchback (1837–1921) was an African American leader of the Republican party in Louisiana during Reconstruction; he served as that state's governor in 1872–73. John Mercer Langston (1829–1917) was a prominent black educator who, in 1890, became the only African American ever elected to the U.S. House of Representatives from Virginia.

saw, too, that when a negro became the owner of a home and was a taxpayer having a regular trade or other occupation, he at once became a conservative and safe citizen and voter; one who would consider the interests of his whole community before casting his ballot; and, further, one whose ballot could not be purchased.

It was at this time that I set out to start an industrial school for the members of my race at the little town of Tuskegee, in what is known as the Black Belt of Alabama.

The first thing I did, as soon as I arrived at the place for establishing the new college, as it was called, was to study the actual needs of the people around it. For this purpose I spent several weeks traveling about in different parts of the county, visiting the colored people in their homes and talking to them in their churches. At the same time I felt compelled to take account of the attitude and disposition of the white people in regard to the new school. I did this because the legislature was furnishing the funds for starting the school and because I saw clearly that there was no hope of putting negro education on a firm basis in the South, unless it was possible to secure the interest and sympathy of the white people. I saw that, if the school I proposed to establish was to be successful, it must find a common ground somewhere between the races. Thus it was that I set out at the very start to secure the support and interest of both white people and black people.

Many people, especially in the North, have a wrong conception of the attitude of the Southern white people towards negro education. It has been very generally thought that what is termed "higher education" of the negro has from the first been opposed by the white South. This opinion is far from correct. I remember that, when I began work at Tuskegee, practically all of the white people who talked to me on the subject took it for granted that instruction in Greek, Latin, and modern languages, would make up the greater part of the curriculum. No one opposed this course of study. In fact, there are many white people in the South today who do not know that instruction in the dead languages is not given at Tuskegee Institute.

The truth is that a large part of the people in the South had little faith in any kind of education for the negro. They were indifferent, but not openly opposed to it. On the other hand, there has always been an influential group of white people in the Southern States who have stood out prominently and courageously for the education of all the people, regardless of race. This group of people has thus far been successful in shaping and directing public opinion, and I think that it will continue to do so more and more. This statement must not be taken to mean that there is as yet an equitable division of the school funds between the two races in all sections of the South, although the Southern States deserve much credit for what has been done.

I wish, however, to emphasize the fact that, while there was open antagonism or indifference in certain directions it was the introduction of industrial training in the negro's education that furnished the first basis for anything like a common interest and united action between the two races in the South, and between the whites in the North and those in the South. Aside from its direct benefit to the black race, industrial education has furnished a basis for mutual confidence and co-operation. And this has meant more to the South, and to the work of education, than has been realized.

From its inception the white people of the South were favorable to industrial education for the negro because they had noted, what was not unnatural, that a large portion of the colored people were disposed immediately after emancipation to interpret freedom to mean freedom from work with the hands. The white people saw in the setting up of schools to teach the negro youth that labor with the hands was honorable, something that would lead the negro into his new life of freedom gradually and prevent him from flying from one extreme of life to the other.

Besides that industrial education appealed directly to the interest of the individual white man and to the community. They saw at once that intelligence, coupled with skill, would add wealth to the community and to the state. Crude labor, in the days of slavery, had been made profitable to a certain extent. The ignorant and unskilled labor, in a state of freedom, could not be made so. Practically every white man in the South was interested directly or indirectly in agriculture or in some other business or trade which employed manual labor. Every white man was interested in all that related to the home life, the cooking and serving of food, laundrying, dairying, poultry raising, and housekeeping generally, so there was a general recognition of the fact that the education of the black people, who had hitherto performed this kind of work, was of vital interest to every white man in the South.

If the black man became a lawyer, a doctor, a minister, or a teacher his professional duty did not under ordinary circumstances bring him into contact, in any direct and vital way, with the life of the white people of the community. The result was that as long as the education of the negro was of a purely literary or professional character it had little interest or significance to the average white man. There was a confused idea that such kind of education might bring about a higher and better type of negro manhood, but that seemed remote and doubtful.

The minute, however, it appeared that as a result of industrial education the negro would not only, for example, study chemistry but apply that chemistry to the enrichment of the soil and the production of crops; apply it to cooking, to dairying, and to other practical matters; the minute it was seen that in the new industrial school the negro was not only learning geometry and physics but applying his knowledge to blacksmithing, brickmaking, house building, and what not; at that moment there began for the first time to be a common bond between the two races and an opportunity for co-operation between the North and the South in the matter of negro education.

It was not so easy to convince the masses of the colored people that there was any virtue in a school that taught their children to work with their hands. They argued, not unnaturally, that they and their people had been worked for 250 years in slavery and now they thought they ought to have a little rest. At any rate, it seemed to them, that a school was the last place on earth where work ought to be so much as mentioned.

I said to them, in reply to these arguments, that it was true that they *had been worked* in slavery; but that now I proposed to teach them *to work*. I said to them that there was a great deal of difference between working and being worked. I said that a man who was worked was a slave but that a man who worked was a free man. I tried to make clear to them that as long as it was necessary to have some one over them to direct, superintend, and follow them up in everything which they did they would remain slaves, but as soon as they learned to work independently, to put skill and intelligence and conscience into their labor then, and not till then, would they become free. It was not easy at first, because of the prejudice that had grown up in slavery against working with the hands, to make the mass of the people see and believe that there was any advantage in having their sons taught to plow and their daughters to cook. They said these things they had done at home and now they wanted them to go to school and learn something new and different.

Nevertheless, the Tuskegee Institute has gone forward year after year, preaching the gospel of the beauty and the dignity of labor and putting it in practice in the shops, in the kitchen, and on the farm. Year by year the number of students has grown as the facilities of the school have increased. Still hundreds of students are turned away every year because we have not room for them in the school grounds. In the meantime, I am glad to say the sentiment with regard to work has completely changed inside the school. Today our students are just as eager to perform the work allotted to them on the farm or in the shop as they are ready to go to a lesson in history, geography, or arithmetic.

At the same time the sentiment towards work has changed among the masses of the colored people outside of the school. In fact I have always believed that the most important service which the Tuskegee Institute has performed, during its thirty years of existence, has been in the direction of changing the sentiment of the masses of the negro people in the South towards the subject of labor with the hands.

LEO M. FAVROT

The Industrial Movement in Negro Rural Schools

1913

Washington's program of "industrial" education had obvious appeal to white school officials and reformers. Washington never viewed his program as a vehicle for making black schools permanently inferior, to be sure, and it became an all-embracing category including various efforts to modernize the long-neglected African American schools. Although many southern whites embraced industrial education as a vehicle for differentiating between white and black education, northern philanthropists used the concept as a way to funnel funds toward improving black schools.

This document, by a southern white, suggests some of the challenges and obstacles that lay in the way of the advocates of an industrial curriculum. Certainly, overwhelming problems of black poverty and white hostility to significant improvement were encountered. In the document, Leo M. Favrot, a native Louisianian who was then serving as state agent for rural schools in Arkansas, reports to the General Education Board about how white school officials and philanthropists perceived the industrial program of improvement for southern black schools.

Spread of the Doctrine of Industrial Education for Negroes

It has only been within the last few years that the white people of the South have begun to realize that the course of study in our elementary

Leo M. Favrot, "The Industrial Movement in Negro Rural Schools," June 9, 1913, Records of the General Education Board, Rockefeller Archive Center, North Tarrytown, N.Y.

schools, as well as in our higher institutions of learning, frequently fails to function properly in the lives of those whom they are trying to educate. We are beginning to realize that our elementary schools for white children have not been fully serving their purpose and that the course of study and direction of the work are still in need of revision. Those of the white race that think at all about the negro education, are even more forcefully impressed with the necessity of providing some form of training in our common schools that will effectually serve the negro boys and girls to do well their work in later years. We of the South have failed until recently to open our eyes to some of the great movements in the South that have long recognized the value of industrial training for negroes. We have not chosen to investigate the work of such an institution as Hampton Institute, Virginia, and are scarcely aware down here in Arkansas of how nearly an institution of this kind is succeeding effectively in solving most of the perplexing questions of our race problem. With Tuskegee Institute, Alabama, and the work of its President, Booker T. Washington, we are a little better acquainted; but those of us that have not fully investigated the matter have no full realization of the scope and power of the influence of these two institutions. Both are trying to train the negro for good citizenship in the South. Both are teaching him such an attitude towards the white man as would enable the two races to live side by side in peace and harmony. Both are laying great stress on the value and dignity of labor and both of these institutions are training the hand and and the heart as well as the head, of their students. When two institutions of this type can boast of the fact that none of its thousands of negro graduates have ever been in jail, we are forced to pay our respects to those charged with the management and direction of their work.

These leading industrial institutions have of course today a great number of followers of lesser magnitude. Those followers that have caught the true spirit that marks the work of Hampton and Tuskegee, are rendering the negro race as well as the South, and the white race in the South, valuable service. It is time that the white man of the South, who has so long been indifferent to the manner of education of the negro, should turn his attention to this problem and work with some vim and zest for such a training of the negro as will effectually build up the South by making of it a land of greater productiveness, a land of law-abiding citizens, and a land of contented humanity.

The Jeanes Fund and Its Use

It may not be generally known that Miss Anna T. Jeanes left her fortune to be used for the education of the negro in the rural districts of the South. This negro school fund was placed in the hands of a board of trustees of seventeen members and Doctor James H. Dillard of New Orleans was made President and Director of the fund. After studying for some time the negro problem in the rural districts of the South, and the best way to make this fund of service to the rural negroes, Doctor Dillard and his associates concluded that the major portion of the fund ought to be spent in providing salaries for supervising industrial teachers and special teachers of industrial subjects to serve in various counties of the southern states; although a small amount of this fund is used to aid in the supplying of better buildings and equipment for the rural districts, some has been used in making school terms longer in certain sections of the South, and some in aid of summer schools and conferences. But the larger portion of the fund has been expended in paying one hundred nineteen supervising industrial teachers in that many counties scattered through thirteen of our southern states. During 1912 over $36,000.00 was spent in paying the salaries of these industrial teachers. It is worthy of note in this connection that in several of the southern states where those supervising teachers have proved their usefulness, the Jeanes Fund no longer pays the entire salary of the teacher but contributes only a part of the necessary salary, the county appropriating the remaining part of the salary and necessary traveling expenses frequently to enable the teacher to visit many schools.

Jeanes Fund Industrial Teachers of Arkansas

Eight counties in Arkansas have been enjoying the benefits of the Jeanes philanthropy during the past year. These counties are: Pulaski, Chicot, Desha, Dallas, Ashley, Arkansas, Jefferson, and Lafayette. In some of these counties, such as Pulaski, the work has been in progress three years. In other counties the work was begun a year ago. Of the industrial teachers at work in Arkansas, five are women and three are men. These teachers have been usually selected for their knowledge of industrial activities appropriate for use in the rural schools as well as for their general attitude towards their own race and the white people of the state and their willingness to do all in their power to raise the standard of living among the negroes. These teachers receive their appointment from the County Superintendent or Examiner and he directs their work. Their salaries are paid by the Jeanes Fund only when this county officer has set his stamp of approval upon their months' work. The teachers are usually employed for eight or nine months at salaries ranging from $40.00 to $50.00 per month.

It is the duty of these teachers to visit as many schools in their county as possible. In these schools they strive to teach the pupils how to sew, how to cook, how to make baskets, how to make various articles out of shucks, oak splits, willow twigs, and other materials, how to make gardens; and they also lecture to the students in the rural schools on cleanliness and personal hygiene. They strive to make them morally better in addition to teaching the students how to work with their hands. These teachers frequently hold meetings among the negro adults talking to them at their school houses and their churches on the advantages of living better lives, of making themselves stronger physically and more able to resist disease. They encourage them to be ambitious to make better crops, to take better care of what they have, and to try to own their own homes. They encourage them to build better houses, to paint their houses, to clean their yards and make them more attractive. In general, they strive to bring as much helpfulness and cheer into every community as is possible. It is hoped that eventually the result of this work will be to give the negroes a better understanding of the activities of country life, enable them to produce more and to conserve more of what they produce, to keep them better satisfied to live in the country and to prevent their crowding to the cities to lead lives of idleness and crime. The effort is, at this time, largely educational but there is little doubt that it will develop into a movement of great social significance.

What Has Been Accomplished

It is rather difficult at this time to name all the definite results of this work. The records of the work do not show in a very definite way what has been done. The fact, however, that we have no knowledge of the exact number of pupils that have been reached or the exact number of negro communities that have been spurred on to greater interest in rural life through the work of these industrial teachers, need not in any manner minimize the effect of their influence and labors. The fact that the teachers of the common schools themselves are not familiar with various forms of industrial activities, has made it rather difficult for the Jeanes Fund teachers to accomplish as much in the way of getting work done by the pupils in the rural schools, as they will accomplish when the common school teachers are more in sympathy with their work and better able to direct such work in their schools. A Jeanes Fund teacher frequently visits a rural school and has each pupil work for an hour or two one day in one week and comes again two weeks later and finds that no work of this kind has been done by the pupils during her absence. Under this condition it is clear that rapid progress cannot be made.

In spite of this handicap, the exhibit of the work done under the direction of the Jeanes Fund teachers in six counties of the state, recently sent to the Conference for Education in the South at Richmond, Virginia, gave ample evidence of the value of this type of work. Many examples of plain sewing — dresses, shirt-waists, aprons, undergarments — samples of fancy sewing, fancy bags, embroidered garments, hemstitched hand-kerchiefs and scarfs of various kinds, drawn work; hand-bags made of cord and attractively lined with silk; watch fobs and necklaces of bead work in fancy designs; a hammock of cord; baskets of willow twigs, shuck mats and shuck mops, split oak baskets and split oak chair bottoms, cane chair bottoms, articles of wood, brooms made of home-grown broom straw — all these represent the various industrial activities illustrated in the exhibits sent to Richmond. It was found impracticable to send articles representing the work in cooking done under the direction of these teachers, but much work of this type has been done in the rural districts.

Perhaps, however, the most valuable contribution that these teachers have made to the cause of popular education in Arkansas, has been in the way of acquainting the colored people and the white people with this kind of work. They are coming more and more to see its practical value and to realize its possibility, both in the way of preparing these pupils in the schools to earn a livelihood and render themselves more efficient indus-trially and in the way of enabling them to become stronger and healthier and better citizens.

One phase of this work that is being stressed to some extent this year is the direction of agricultural club work among the boys and girls by these industrial teachers. Several of them have assisted the United States Farm Demonstration agents in organizing Boys Corn and Cotton Clubs and Girls Tomato Clubs among the negro boys and girls.[1] At a recent meeting of the Canning Club agents in Little Rock, two of these industrial teachers attended the sessions and received the benefits of demonstration in can-ning. These two women, Mattie Johnson and Edmonia Parker, came to Little Rock at their own expense because they are genuinely interested in their work and want to make themselves as serviceable as possible.

The Work of the State Supervisor

The fact that the industrial work among the negro schools in the state was not as wide-spread as is desired, and the further fact that it was found

---

[1] The GEB, working through Seaman A. Knapp, had earlier financed agricultural demonstration agents who were instrumental in introducing and popularizing methods of scientific agriculture and farm management. Under the Smith-Lever Act (1914), with the establishment of the county extension service, Knapp's system of agricultural extension came under federal control.

difficult under the former system to give this work careful direction and supervision, have led to the employment of a State Supervisor of rural schools for negro industrial work. The General Education Board of New York City came forward with an appropriation to supply this new office. It is the duty of the State Supervisor to strive to call attention to the manifold advantages of this type of work in the rural districts. He would endeavor to systematize the work where it is already installed, and to advocate its introduction in those counties of the state where it is not yet known. He will gather statistics on negro education in the state and will do all he can to assist the county superintendents and directors in making these schools as truly efficient as possible. He will constantly co-operate with school and county authorities and with the industrial teachers themselves to this end.

Realizing the necessity for having the common school rural teacher in full sympathy and understanding with the real aims and purposes of the rural school, the State Supervisor has been actively engaged in providing for the operation of five industrial Summer Normal Schools for negro teachers. These schools will be operated during the month of June and in addition to offering the regular common school Academic subjects, will offer courses in as many lines of industry as is found practicable. County superintendents and examiners and directors have been urged to send the negro teachers to these Summer Schools and it is hoped that school authorities and teachers will respond to the urgent need of becoming better acquainted with the plan for rendering more efficient the rural schools for negroes in the state of Arkansas. A full attendance at these Normal Schools will insure the rapid spread of industrial activities into the rural district schools. And this means the beginning of a better day for the rural districts.

Possibilities in the Work

It is difficult to estimate the possibilities in this industrial movement among the negroes in rural communities. The fact that Hampton and Tuskegee and other institutions of lesser renown have succeeded so well in industrializing the lives of their graduates among the negro race, should give us encouragement in our efforts to carry into remote rural districts of Arkansas, some of this work. The fact that the great mass of the negroes in our rural districts is ignorant is no argument in favor of leaving them in ignorance. Under the industrial system that prevailed in slavery times the negroes were not left in ignorance, but were carefully trained along industrial lines. In those days the individual slave-holder assumed a responsibility which in our day and time the state can ill-afford to shun. In those days it was to the interest of the slave-holder to train the slave negro to become efficient. It is no less to the interest of the South today to train the negro for efficiency. When the forces over this country that are working for better health conditions, unite with those concerned with moral reform, and these two work harmoniously with the powers that direct a greater industrial and agricultural production, we have a powerful combination of forces working for the betterment of humanity generally. But when these three elements are made the basis of the course of study in the common schools, and are recognized by the educational forces as of equal importance at least with the three R's, then will the school begin truly to serve its real purpose. And finally when it is recognized throughout the South that the negro is here to stay and that the best thing to do for him is to make him as efficient and useful, as healthy and as decent as possible, then will we truly be at work on the problem of really educating all the children of all the people to their highest possible measure of individual efficiency, to the end that our Southland may see an era of more wide-spread prosperity and contentment than has yet been known to us.

6

New Women

Women filled the ranks of racial moderates and reformers, prohibition-ists, child-labor campaigners, school reformers, and public health enthu-siasts, and they became leaders and foot soldiers of Progressive Era social reforms everywhere in the United States. By about 1910, southern women increasingly questioned their traditional roles, which excluded them from politics and voting. Many of them joined another reform campaign — a votes-for-women crusade. Although not all reformers be-came supporters of woman suffrage — or "suffragists" — virtually all suffragists had a background in reform. Woman suffrage was thus both a political movement and an important dimension of southern social reform.

Many of the leading suffragists came from socially elite families. The most prominent suffragists of the pre–World War I era — Madeline McDowell Breckinridge of Kentucky, Pattie Ruffner Jacobs of Alabama, Lila Meade Valentine of Virginia, and Minnie Fisher Cunningham of Texas — hailed from at least middle-class backgrounds from the urban South. Each of these women exhibited exceptional leadership talents and had a strong background as an activist. They were convinced that social reform was impossible without the enfranchisement of women. Twentieth-century women wanted the vote, Madeline McDowell Breck-inridge said in 1913, because of "changed conditions" that had extended the role of women into the world. This new role did not mean the destruction of married women's role with the family; many suffragists, after all, were married with traditional roles as wives and mothers. By demanding the vote, Breckinridge maintained, women were not so much abandoning their traditional roles as they were "demanding a share" of the management of public policy.[1]

Woman suffrage organizations were established in the South as early as the 1880s, and by the 1890s there were suffragists across the region.

[1] Breckinridge, speech before the Virginia legislature, 1913, Papers of the Breckinridge Family, Library of Congress, Washington, D.C.

Many were active participants in the national campaign for enfranchising women that was led by the National American Woman Suffrage Association. But not until after about 1910 did a wider mobilization of southern suffragism — energized by involvement in a wide array of social reforms — occur. Between 1910 and 1915, southern suffrage organizations led campaigns to pass woman suffrage by legislative enactment or constitutional amendment, without success. The woman suffrage crusade did not end, however; during the next four years the movement gained even wider support.

The emergence of "new" women in the South crossed racial lines. By the 1890's, middle-class African American women had organized themselves in women's clubs and had begun to participate in social reforms around the South. As the Margaret Murray Washington document suggests (see p. 135), black reforming women had high expectations but constantly confronted the limitations of Jim Crow. As in other reforms, although white women reformers believed in the uplift of women generally, they only rarely abandoned a belief in white supremacy. Some white women suffragists went further, arguing that votes-for-women should be a whites-only phenomenon. Granting white women the vote, according to one Mississippi suffragist, would guarantee "immediate and durable white supremacy, honestly attained."[2]

The views of two prominent suffragists, novelist Mary Johnston of Virginia (see p. 141) and Rebecca Latimer Felton of Georgia (see p. 147), show that suffragists did not escape prevailing class and cultural assumptions. But these documents also suggest that the campaign for woman suffrage had far-reaching implications, for women reformers saw it as an attempt to reshape the traditional southern family. Because legislatures were elected by male-only constituencies, suffragists argued, they had fashioned a public policy without the interests of women and children in mind. Suffragists often pointed to age-of-consent laws that established minimum ages for sexual intercourse. Georgia's age-of-consent law, which in the early 1900s was set at ten, demonstrated that the legal code was, according to one woman reformer, "dictated solely by men." When the Mississippi legislature refused in 1914 to raise the age of consent from twelve to eighteen, a suffragist lamented that there was no stronger argument for woman suffrage than this "disgraceful fact."[3]

After 1915, the suffrage fight focused on the adoption of a federal constitutional amendment, the Nineteenth Amendment, to grant women

[2] Belle Kearney, "Race Problem in the South," *Augusta (Ga.) Tribune,* Apr. 22, 1903.
[3] H. Augusta Howard, "A Stinging Rebuke for Atlanta's Pharisees," *Woman's Tribune,* Dec. 5, 1891; reprint, *New Orleans Item,* 1914.

the right to vote. Yet the campaign for national legislation caused a major split among southern suffragists — a large portion of whom opposed any federal action — and occasioned the emergence of an antisuffrage campaign. Thus, when the U.S. House of Representatives endorsed the amendment in January 1918, 90 of the 101 votes cast in opposition were from southern congressmen, and both houses adopted the measure only after strong resistance from southern members from both the House and Senate. Like other social reformers, southern suffragists discovered strong resistance to woman suffrage as they took the campaign to ratify the amendment to the people in 1919–20. Although Tennessee, in August 1920, became the thirty-sixth — and last — state to ratify the Nineteenth Amendment, only four other ratifying states (Arkansas, Kentucky, Oklahoma, and Texas) were southern states. Put another way, of the ten states in the Union that refused to ratify or, in some cases, to consider the suffrage amendment, only one, Delaware, lay above the Mason-Dixon line.

When reading the documents in this chapter, consider the following questions:

1. In what respects do the views of these woman suffragists resemble those of other southern social reformers?

2. To what extent does the African American woman reformer Margaret Murray Washington share the attitudes of the white reformers Mary Johnston and Rebecca Latimer Felton?

3. To what extent are these woman suffragists traditionalists in their views about the family? In what respects are they nontraditionalists?

4. To what extent are these woman suffragists similar to other reformers in their views on race? In their views on culture?

MARGARET MURRAY WASHINGTON

The Gain in the Life of Negro Women

1904

Born in Macon, Georgia, Margaret Murray Washington (1865–1925) was a black woman reformer and the third wife of Booker T. Washington. A graduate of Fisk University, Margaret Murray became "lady principal" at Tuskegee in 1890, a position that she kept even after her marriage a year later. Following her marriage to Booker T. Washington in 1891, she helped to form the Tuskegee Woman's Club in 1895, and thereafter she figured significantly in the black women's club movement. In 1896, she helped to found the National Federation of Afro-American Women, which represented thirty-six black women's clubs in twelve states. This organization later became a part of the newly organized National Association of Colored Women, of which Margaret Murray Washington served as president from 1912 to 1918.

In this document, Washington describes the status of African American women, especially reforming middle-class black women.

In the many-tongued discussion of negro problems there is no fallacy so common or so insidious as that by which a proposition found true of a particular group of negroes is, in virtue of that fact, proclaimed true of all or of the great mass. To maintain that since from the negroes in a certain town no superior class has emerged, the negroes of America have no superior class — to maintain that is to feel with the Africans that, because the white slave-catchers were merciless, all white men are merciless. The specific problem which is the subject of this paper — Gain in the Life of Negro Women — is often similarly befuddled. There are 8,840,789 negroes in this country, of whom 4,447,568 are women. These women live in States from Massachusetts to Mississippi; some live on plantations, some in towns, some in cities; some are ignorant, some intelligent; some are rich, some poor; some good, some bad. To make propositions that will hold true of these many and essentially different groups of negro women is a task which I do not essay — a task to which Edmund Burke referred when he said that no man can indict a whole race of people.

Margaret Murray Washington, "The Gain in the Life of Negro Women," *Outlook* 71 (Jan. 30, 1904): 271–74.

Moreover, you can no more find the "average" negro woman than you can multiply eggs by treaties. Just as eggs are different from treaties, so good negro women are different from bad negro women, and no average can be struck. The best we can do is to estimate the size of the various groups of negro women, but even this is not enough; the influence, efficiency, significance of one superior woman's life may be indefinitely more than that of ten dull drudges. And so the statistical method could not do justice to this essentially human problem; statistics negate individuality.

I propose to speak of the superior class of negro women, and roughly to indicate something of the import of their organized endeavor.

Every census teems with information that testifies to the material and spiritual gain of the negro population and notably of negro women. To cite a few illustrations from school enrollment, I may say that in the census year 1,096,774 negroes attended school, of whom 510,007 were males and 586,767 were females; 27,858 females as against 28,268 males attended school from two to three months; 160,231 females as against 136,028 males attended school from four to five months; and 227,546 females as against 187,173 males attended school six months and more. These figures indicate the well-known fact that girls attend school more continuously than boys; the boys must go to work while the girls are in school.

In the one hundred public high schools for negroes, 3,659 girls as against 2,974 boys were enrolled in elementary grades, and in secondary grades 3,933 girls and 1,634 boys. In these schools 154 girls were enrolled in the business course; 792 in the classical course; 1,098 girls in the scientific course. In the normal course of the high schools there were 221 girls and 65 boys. In the industrial training courses there were 709 girls and 550 boys. 501 girls and 177 boys graduated in 1900–1 from the high-school course.

In the secondary and higher schools of the colored race there were 13,306 females and 9,587 males in elementary grades; 7,383 females and 6,164 males in the secondary grades; 740 females and 2,339 males in the collegiate course. In secondary and higher schools there were 17,138 colored students receiving the industrial training, of whom 11,012 were females.

These young negro women have not come through the schools on "flowery beds of ease." While their mothers and fathers of the generation of yesterday have not been able to give them that home training essential to the best development, they have by the sweat of their brows aided their boys and girls to get the education for which they themselves had yearned in vain. The average young negro woman has either helped her parents on the cotton patch or her mother with her laundry work, during vacation, and in that way has helped to defray her expenses through school. The large majority have worked their way through school in spite of the heavy odds against them. Better home training might have aided them the better to meet the problems confronting them in their lives and service.

At any rate, the schools are each year appreciably increasing the number of educated women of negro blood. The educational provision is of course dangerously inadequate; thus, I know of a great Southern State where there has not for years been a nearly sufficient number of candidates for positions as teachers who could meet the minimum requirements. However, the proportion of educated negro women to-day is very much greater than in 1860. The crucial question is always whether, in the environment in which the negro school or college girl eventually finds herself, she will be able to maintain in her life the ideals of school and college. A superior class of negro women, realizing this situation, have organized a system of clubs to meet the difficulty in some measure. The educated negro girl, these women say, must not go back to the blanket! The woman's club organizes the social life of educated negro women on rational principles, and urges those women to intelligent social service. From this point of view, and from many others, the club movement is interesting.

The club movement among negro women, with social betterment as the aim, began fifteen years ago. So educative was the force that a National Association was organized in 1895. To-day West Virginia, Ohio, Iowa, Pennsylvania, Illinois, Missouri, Mississippi, and Alabama have State federations. The Northeastern Federation of forty-five clubs confines its work to the Northeast. The Southern Federation of two hundred and twenty-five clubs is devoted to work in the Southern States, but its clubs are affiliated with the National organization.

The work of the individual club is varied. The largest of these have departments directed by women interested in certain phases of uplift — free kindergartens, day nurseries, temperance, prison work, social purity, Mothers' Unions, and the like. The intellectual development has an outlet by discussions of live topics. Here is a typical evening's programme of one of these clubs:

Music, Vocal.
Russia, Past and Present.
Quartet.
The Representative People of Russia.

Life of the Russian Peasant Women as Compared with that of Negro
　　Women.
Instrumental Music.

Our women are wide awake to the necessity of social culture, and no
more pleasing feature is there than to receive their friends in their best
attire in tastefully furnished reception-rooms. This is a diversion on the
club programme perhaps once a year. But the earnest, faithful work of
these women in their chosen fields of labor is the aim of their existence.
By their efforts free kindergartens, day nurseries, sewing and cooking
schools, are supported. Hundreds of untaught mothers living with their
children in their cabin homes or in the crowded tenements of the cities
are taught how to live. In some of the large towns weekly meetings are
held with an average attendance of one hundred and fifty women. Helpful
talks are given on such subjects as:

How to Keep Close to the Children.
How to Keep the Confidence of Children.
Mother's Authority in Selecting Company for the Children.
How a Mother can Help her Daughter to Avoid Mistakes as Regards
　　the Young Man she Loves.
White Cross Leagues for Boys.
Relation of Brother and Sister.
Teaching a Boy to Protect Women.

In the conferences that follow, many a revolution is promised that tells
that the hints have struck home. House-to-house visits show that progress is made. Where crowded conditions have not seemed to promote a
healthy moral atmosphere, attempts have been made to gain privacy by
a simple screen device, and in many instances this has been a spur to save
money and buy homes. These Mothers' Unions or Conferences are
training-schools for social betterment, and the cities, towns, and settlements of the plantations all over the South are giving evidences of these
helpful influences brought to bear on the lives of our women belonging
to the generation of yesterday.

For the past five years the Southern Federation of Colored Women's
Clubs has met in the cities of Montgomery, Alabama; Atlanta, Georgia;
Vicksburg, Mississippi; New Orleans, Louisiana; and recently in Jacksonville, Florida. After each yearly meeting the impetus gained in the work
has been wonderful. Club life has a strong hold in all the cities and States
of the South. Each year the new accessions come better prepared to lend
a hand in the service. Mothers, business women, school-teachers, are

equally active in their efforts to reach out after those who should be awakened to the necessity of proper home making and training for their children.

In the story of the evolution of a club woman in one of our periodicals the trend of the club idea of the white woman seems to take her away from home duties. But our negro women are American daughters of aliens whose home life has not generations of culture behind it, and our work must be practical.

Yet a large percentage of our negro women preside in homes of their own in all these cities where the Southern Federation of Negro Women's Clubs has been privileged to meet. The majority of these club women have helped their husbands to purchase homes by their thrift and economy. Many of these residences are situated on prominent streets. They are well-designed, painted cottages of six and eight rooms, with bath and hot and cold water contrivances, well ventilated, and constructed with an eye to sanitary arrangements. These homes are tastefully furnished.

The hostesses who have entertained the delegations of the Federation as the years have passed, not only know how to keep house, but how to cook and serve well-prepared meals properly in well-appointed dining-rooms. The same women have attended the daily sessions of the conventions, and are those who give the addresses of welcome, direct the federated clubs of the city, and conduct those Mothers' Conferences that are proving vital helps. These women are the leaders in the side trips, trolley rides, and local receptions given as recreations to the visiting workers. They are women following their chosen pursuits — dressmaking, millinery, manicuring. They are clerks, stenographers, trained nurses, teachers, workers in every field of labor that helps them to make a living and buy homes. In many of our largest cities a goodly percentage of the bank depositors are negro women. This means a nest-egg for the purchase and ownership of homes. The negro women are unmodern in that they assume a share in working to pay for homes for their families. In many instances young married couples unite their savings in buying homes — in this order of helpmate may lie some of the reason for gain in the sacredness of the marriage tie.

From all these club centers of the South there radiates over each State an influence that has caused marked improvement in the home life of women gaining instruction in domestic affairs from the club conferences to which they belong.

I have emphasized the educative force of the club, because it has been by this means, certainly, that the passing generation of negro women has been able to meet the demands of family responsibilities.

Young negro women of to-day are developing under fairer conditions. The home training combined with the school training of head, hand, and heart develops that steadiness of purpose that underlies strong, sturdy character.

Our young woman is already taking her place in various spheres of life, regardless of precedent. Her training fits her for home life and the larger social service of the school-room. She does with her might what her hands find to do. A college girl directs a steam laundry or makes soap in a large laundering establishment. She has spent four years at Greek and Latin, but has charge of a broom factory where girls are manufacturing brooms of all sorts and sizes. She has gained all the training possible in the schools of her native heath, and by arduous sacrifice has worked her way through the best New England schools of domestic science that she might be thoroughly prepared to teach. She has a laboratory for her theory classes in cooking. She teaches practical cooking daily to large classes of white-capped, white-aproned girls, with individual towels and holders, and at the end of each week in one school alone four hundred and fifty negro girls have learned to cook by doing. No more helpful encouragement has come for this work than the testimonials from white women of the South interested in the improvement of some of these girls.

Young negro women are teaching hundreds of their sisters the same principles of dressmaking and millinery that they were taught in the training-schools of Pratt and Teachers' College. And these young women are not misfits. They are not despondent in their calling. They are putting in brain with the would-be drudgery, and are making marked success of industries where women with fewer advantages might have failed to show their pupils the true dignity of labor.

The present indications of advance in the life of negro women are most hopeful for the future of the race. With the home training that is becoming possible, with the training that our schools afford, with the inheritance of true worth that made the parents do their utmost to bequeath to their children honest, upright lives, the young negro women will possess that wealth of character that will be the means eventually of dispelling the greatest barriers that may confront the race.

Whether or not we attribute this gain to school, club, or religious influence, we do know that much is due to the club, and we know that the future of the race is dependent upon the women and their standards of living. Whatever force is at work that is developing that strength of character which is the bulwark of an individual or race, we hope it will obtain a permanent hold in the life of negro women.

It remains with the greater mass of our women to make the weal or woe come quickly or linger. But the signs of the times are bright. The educative forces are at work. The greater mass is being leavened, and we thank God that there will be no retrograde. There has been none and there will be none!

MARY JOHNSTON

Speech

May 31, 1910

Born in 1870 in Buchanan, Virginia, Mary Johnston is best known as the author of twenty-three novels, a number of which, such as To Have and to Hold *(1898), were great commercial successes. Some of her novels, such as* Hagar *(1913), dealt with feminist themes, and by the time of World War I, Johnston was involved in a variety of reform efforts. Johnston was also a leading suffragist, and in 1909 she helped to found the Equal Suffrage League of Virginia, an organization that campaigned aggressively over the next decade to obtain votes for Virginia women.*

Like other women reformers, Johnston saw woman suffrage as the natural extension of social reforms in which women were deeply involved. In this document, she describes her conception of the connections between the expanding influence that women had had with Progressive Era social reform and the need to provide for woman suffrage.

. . . The twentieth century will be called the Woman's Century. Why will it be called that? It will be called that for one thing because it is producing and will produce more and more a very noble type of woman — free women and noble. It will be called that because for the first time in thousands of years women will be in the majority in all the more specifically sociological, humane, and educational aspects of human society. Already they are in the majority. It will be called that because women are becoming artists and administrators, writers, scientists, educators, histo-

Mary Johnston, speech, May 31, 1910, Papers of Mary Johnston, Manuscripts Department, University of Virginia Library.

rians, poets. It will be called that because, before this century closes, women will have become economically independent. It will be called that because, before the first quarter of the century closes, she will, over a great part of the western world have gained her political freedom. Before 1950 strikes, with the exception possibly of some of the more backward Latin peoples, she will have wholly gained it. It will be called that because it is the great, the revolutionary century, because it is the woman's century.

Why do we desire the franchise? How idle a question is this. But since we answer children, let us also answer this. Let us answer it like Alice in Wonderland with another question. Why did men want it? Presumably because they found it to their highest and best interests. . . . Self-protection, self-government, self-development, self-realization — those are the ideas associated from the beginning with that concept, political liberty.

When we have answered as above, we have answered to the point and with fullness. The statement is incontrovertible, unanswerable. It is comprehensive. It is sufficient. But we may point out, if it is wished, some details included in the whole.

Protection and fair play for the economic woman — for the millions of women workers out in the world of industry, dis-franchised as Chinese coolies! They need the protection of that ballot — oh, they need it, they need it! Witness the shirtwaist-maker's strike in New York, last year! . . . Witness the long, long hours of the women in factory, mill, and shop! Witness the long struggle of women teachers for equal pay for equal work. Witness the starvation wage that sends young girls upon the street! Witness the lack of inspection, the lack of safety appliances. Witness the tenement crowding, witness the sweat shop! Witness child labour! Witness the White Slave traffic![1] Witness a thousand things!

We wish the franchise for the sake of some control over all the multitudinous aspects of an industrial civilization. . . . We wish it because we are taxed without representation, and governed without consent. We wish it because there are forces of corruption which threaten our existence and our happiness, and the existence and happiness of our children, and we now stand before these forces with bound hands! We wish it for the sake of a voice in the environment of home, in the character of the government of the city, the state, the United States! We wish it as educated women, not agreeing to the closing of all higher social functions to us, because we were born women! We wish it as taxpayers, helping to

---

[1] "White slave traffic" was a term commonly used to describe the commercial system of prostitution. Anti-vice reformers maintained that prostitutes were victims of a system that enslaved them.

run the government, and not allowed a voice in government. We wish it as humanitarians, desiring an injection into affairs of far, far more love for our fellow beings. We wish it as eugenists,[2] fighting for the welfare of the present race, fighting the production of a far nobler, finer, higher human type. From an undeveloped mother cannot spring a developed race. We wish it because we wish aroused a dormant power in women, because we wish to see humanized and socialized a womanhood that has been hitherto too individualistic, because we wish slowly to lift the mother of the race to a clime and air where she may bear great sons and great daughters. We wish it as women with love and feeling for our sister women. Too long, too long have women held apart from women! What is man's strongest asset? The fraternal instinct. Ages and ages ago, began that which he can and does rely upon today! Men banded themselves together, first to hunt, then to fight. Hunting band, war party — they taught him the manual of shoulder-to-shoulder, of hand in hand, of co-operative strength, subordination of the will of one to the good of all, fellowship, comradeship! All through the ages men have marched together, hunted and fought together, worked together, suffered together. It has humanized them, socialized them, taught them brotherhood. — But for ages and ages and ages from the fall of the matriarchate to the present period, woman as woman has been segregated, isolated. She has lived apart from millions of her sisters; she has missed the fraternal instinct. You see there is not even a feminine word to match "fraternal." She has the most powerful of assets in the maternal instinct, the strongest of all assets, far outweighing in might and in depth the man's paternal feeling. But she has missed the instinct of sisterhood. This great integrating movement, the woman's movement, is correcting that. It is giving to woman a new feeling, impulse, motive, possession — it is giving her sisterhood.

We ask the franchise in the interests of Justice, in the interests of truth, of Enlightenment, of thought, of altruism. We ask it in the interests of the whole of the human race, of man, of woman, of child. In fighting the battle of the half we are fighting the battle of the whole.

If the position of woman, today, is abnormal, then the position of man also is abnormal. It will be better for us both to travel on the plane of Justice, on the good high road to Fair Play. We are all intelligent people here. I am not going to spend much time on the stock objections to the franchise for women. They are old. There are no new ones. They are

---

[2] The eugenics movement, which enjoyed a peak of popularity worldwide during the first third of the twentieth century, sought to develop a "science" by which races could be improved through the improvement of their hereditary qualities.

perfectly shop worn. They have done duty against every reform, every lightening of the burden of discriminatory law and custom which woman has borne and yet bears. The education of women at all — the higher education of women — the married woman's property act — equal guardianship laws — one and all have met the same old war cries. We will look for a moment or two, however, at two or three of these perfectly conventional objections, these catchwords that people pick up and throw as idly as a boy throws a rock.

It will not work. But it is working. It is working all the time. It is working like a great heart beat — like this! It has been working in Wyoming for forty years, in Colorado for seventeen, in Australia and New Zealand for sixteen, in Norway and Sweden for years. The mind that makes that statement does not know what it is talking about. It is much as if a man should say, "I hear that a fellow named Morse has invented a thing called a telegraph, but it won't work."

It will work badly. Well, maybe it will for some forces of evil, some forces of exploitation. But in its large aspect, and for the nobler forces it does not work badly. It works well. The testimony as to this is overwhelmingly great, and overwhelmingly trust worthy.

Women as a class are already represented by men as a class. That is not true, and no thinking man or woman thinks that it is true.

Women can obtain what they wish by indirect influence. When serious people seriously discuss the faults of men as men and of the faults of women as women what, in the latter case, is almost the first thing they begin upon? The indirect way in which women approach the end they wish to achieve. There are few phrases more distasteful to a naturally self-respecting and straightforward woman than that phrase "indirect influence." She hears it from many lips. It means *Make me comfortable, and I will see what I can do about it.* Do you know, people often take up with catch phrases and spurious reasons without in the very least examining their meaning? They are always given to them by someone else. They never originate them. They simply repeat them and pass them on — to do harm again. This is one of those arguments. It seems to me that as a people we might wish to see indirection left out of our women's makeup. It seems to me that it would be wiser, nobler, and more filled with promise for the great human type we wish to see evolved to let that phrase "indirect influence" drop into the past.

When women are politically free men will become less chivalrous. That is another catch phrase, and it is usually put forward by those who would be hard put to it to give a definition of chivalry. I think that a little observation will show you that the truly chivalrous man does not use it, and neither does the true gentlewoman. Gentleness of heart and courtesy, quickness to see injustice and to right it, good manners, and good will will not disappear from the earth upon the happy day when women are politically free and there is on earth one injustice the less! We forget that chivalry, neither, is a thing of sex. The woman who is courteous and helpful, quick to see a wrong and to right it, strong to help the weak and uplift the fallen — she also is chivalrous. It seems to me that women like Jane Addams and Florence Kelley are very good knights. Sunshine does not kill sunshine, and light and liberty and justice will not put out of commission true knightliness. They are the things the true knights are fighting for. Last year at the Capitol I heard more talk in one day about chivalry from the lawyer in the pay of the knitting mills who were under indictment for overworking women and children than you would perhaps have heard from Bayard or Sir Philip Sidney in a year. I should, personally, be doubtful of the quality of the chivalry that is going to be so utterly extinguished by an amendment to the Constitution.

Only the bad women will vote. Or even if the good women vote, there are so many bad women that they will put out of commission the good women. In the last analysis by the undesirable woman is meant the prostitute. One half of one percent of the women of America. One in two hundred . . . That statement angers me, whether it may be made by a man or by a woman. In the case of the man it is a little more cowardly, in the case of the woman a little more traitorous. In both cases it is alike false and silly. . . . We will not dwell upon this objection but leave it to be thrashed out by those of both sexes who know so many bad women.

It is a change. Granted. It is a change, and a long needed one. I doubt if any of us realize how many ills of society, how many diseases of the body politic are due to the fact that change was not made long, long ago!

Our forefathers did not have it. No, nor several other things that we possess. For one thing, they didn't have our world. For another they didn't have our economic conditions. For a third they didn't have our minds. As a woman thinketh, so she is. There is not one of us here today who could stand in that terrible past. Not a day passes but we say that, think that, and do that for which three hundred years ago we might have been burned in the market place. We see no reason: we see only babe-like folly and ignorance in the statement that because the grandparents had not liberty the grandchildren must not strive for nor win it!

Women are not required to trouble their heads about public affairs. Of old, in Sparta, no one was allowed to be indifferent in matters of common weal. Was such and such a question agitated among the people? — pro and con? Then, under penalty, you must take sides. No citizen was allowed to say, "I am too busy to bother about it," or "It isn't in my sphere," or "Am I my brother's keeper?" Sparta said, "This is a matter that touches us all. If you haven't got an opinion, go, form one! If you are too stupid to form one, you are too stupid to be a citizen of Sparta. We will declare you idiot and disfranchise you!" There was no such thing as being on the fence in Sparta. The fence, in that sense, didn't exist. . . . There were some excellent things about Sparta.

Women are too prompted by their emotions, too sentimental for affairs. . . . Do you know, I am not at all sure that we are the sentimental sex? But allowing it to be so for the sake of argument — Last year I was talking to a man in Washington. He was — oh, he was a violent anti-suffragist! He was extreme. And that was the burden of his cry, "Women are creatures of emotion! They are actuated by sentiment. Give them the vote and behold a nation swayed by sentiment!" We left the subject; I didn't see any use pursuing it. And then we got to talking amicably upon politics in general and business — politics ruthless and greedy, cold, hard, unfeeling business! Those were his terms, not mine. "It is all a heartless, calculating game!" he said. "What do politics and business as conducted in this country today care for the genuine interests of the people? It's all a heartless game! I tell you, Miss Johnston, what this country needs is sentiment in public life!" . . . I used to think that men were great logicians.

Women cannot fight. Well, this is hardly true. In all lands and ages women have fought, fought with bare hands, fought with what weapons they could lay their hands upon, fought to protect their children, fought to protect their virtue. But grant that the actual bearing of arms by women in case of war is not under consideration. Neither is it for men over forty-five, and yet they vote. No man who is not physically robust is required to give military service, and yet he votes. All men who are serving the state in civic positions, all teachers, all clergymen, etc., these are exempt from military duty and yet they vote. . . . And in case of war do not women act as a great reserve force? Do they not nurse, do they not gather and forward supplies, do they not keep the home, the farm, the town, the children, the sick, the old, the wounded? In a thousand ways do they not give military service? In our war were not the women as patriotic as the men, and did not the South owe as much perhaps to her women as to the soldiers in the field? General Joseph E. Johnston said of one Southern woman that she was worth to the service a brigade.

In the United States approximately five thousand women die every year in giving life to men and women. More women have died in child birth since the war than died soldiers on both sides during the war. More women have died in giving life than have died soldiers in all the wars that have ever been fought. "Women," says someone, "do not bear arms, but they bear armies." Lucy Stone said, "Some woman risks her life whenever a soldier is born into the world. For years she does picket duty beside his cradle. Later on she is his quartermaster and gathers his supplies. And when that boy grows to be a man, shall he say to his mother, 'If you want to vote, you must first go and kill somebody!' It is a coward's argument."

REBECCA LATIMER FELTON

The Subjection of Women and the Enfranchisement of Women

1915

A noted southern reformer and suffragist, Rebecca Latimer Felton (1835–1930) spent her entire life in Georgia. As a widow in the 1870s, she became active in women's benevolence and temperance organizations in Cartersville, in the northwest section of the state. Active in the efforts of the unsuccessful political campaigns of her husband, the physician and Populist William Harrell Felton, by the 1890s Rebecca Latimer Felton was a well-known activist in campaigns against the convict lease system — in which prisoners were subject to horrific conditions while working for private contractors — and for Prohibition. On other issues, such as child-labor restriction, Felton parted company with reformers; in a famous controversy in 1891, she defended Georgia cotton mill owners against the charge of mistreatment of children. Like other southern reformers, Felton combined her reformism with virulent racism. In 1897, for example, she defended lynching as a tool to control black rapists.

By 1900, Felton was a dedicated suffragist, and this document explains her general views on suffrage and feminism.

… Every sane and sensible reader of current events is already convinced that the march of progress will bring equality in the rights of citizenship to

Rebecca Latimer Felton, *The Subjection of Women and the Enfranchisement of Women* (Cartersville, Ga.: 1915).

every State in the Union — time enough being given. In the year 1912, four millions of women were entitled to vote in County, State, and National elections. This privilege was given them by the men voters of nine States and one territory. In 1914, under most unfavorable conditions, two other States were added to the enfranchised States. For many years, partial suffrage for women has been granted by the men voters in other partially enfranchised States. In every case it has been accomplished by the votes of men; and the result has been enthusiastically approved by the Governors, Senators, and representatives of those free States. For lack of space I must omit these commendations at this time, but I have the data in hand and whenever my statements are disputed I will make suitable reply. There can be no retreat in this war. While the opposition is often rabid and in a manner insulting to those who see the end from the beginning and who have the courage to express their honest and well substantiated convictions, we remember it is always so in reform movements. Twenty odd years ago, when Georgia was full of bar-rooms and liquor distilleries — I dared to go, upon request, to various towns and cities in Georgia and demand protection from the destruction that walked in darkness and wasted at noonday — and which destroyed thousands of Georgia homes — and crucified the hopes of tens of thousands of mothers and wives in our own state. I was not only fought by those who were making fortunes out of the liquor traffic, but by politicians and even churchmen. I was often warned as to what would happen to me if I persisted. To-day, it is expected that temperance women shall publicly debate this subject, hold temperance prayer-meetings, and openly oppose (with their limited influence) every liquor candidate for office. I have had knowledge of these things and I have decided that this terrible thing was voted in upon us by "big interests" and can only be voted out by giving the ballot to women — who are the chief victims. *Woman Suffrage had its inception in this fight against Saloons.* The W.C.T.U., the National Organization, is pledged to Woman Suffrage. . . .

Former Subjection of Women

Savage tribes used physical force to manage their women. The club and the lash were their only arguments. Moslem fanatics went a step further in saying women have no souls. According to statistics these Mohammedans comprise about one-third of such religionists at this time. Athenian law allowed a man to sell his wife or sister under certain conditions. Federal law allowed men to imprison their sisters in convents — while they used the property that was rightfully their sisters — in riotous living.

English law, in the time of Herbert Spencer,[1] allowed a man to beat his wife, and he could lock her in any room in his house, and keep her imprisoned until her will was subdued to his own. English law was copied by the Colonies of America. Lawyers will tell you now, that English law has been the basic stone of our laws — State and Federal. As late as the year 1857, a man in Georgia was allowed to beat his wife, provided the hickory withe was no larger than his thumb. I wish I knew the Georgian's name who introduced the bill for a married woman's relief in 1857, three years before secession. I would like to contribute to a fund to place a suitable tablet to his memory in our State Capitol.

As late as 1868 a Supreme Court Judge in North Carolina reiterated the law allowing a man to beat his wife, with a rod no bigger than his thumb. In his verdict (on a wife beating case) he said a man should make his wife behave herself, otherwise it would *"engender insubordination."*

A woman in Georgia could not own her own wages — as late as 1897. Hon. W. H. Fleming introduced the bill to allow a married woman to receive and spend what she earned outside her home. Before that time "her man" could demand them from her employer on pain of compelling him to pay twice, and he could spend them where he pleased, in a dram shop or gambling den, or bawdy house — and she could not recover them to her own use. Before the Civil War, a married woman in Georgia could not own her own clothes. When she went to her new home she might carry a fortune in lands and slaves, but she did not really own a copper cent of their value. Thousands of slaves and lands belonging to ante-bellum women were sold for the husband's security debts. Sometimes her first information was received when the sheriff came to dispossess her. Sometimes a marriage contract was required by anxious parents, but the woman was made to suffer for it. I knew a young woman who declined a marriage contract, because her fiance told her it would be a reflection on himself and it would "break his heart" to be thus distrusted. Nevertheless he proved himself faithless — in mind, morals, and her estate. A woman cannot practice law in Georgia today, no matter how well prepared by study and genius. There are scores of women doctors — but our legislators draw a line at the law.

Before the war[2] *her only chance lay in her foresight in accepting or finding for herself a good master.* I have known the same privilege extended to favorite slaves — who were forced to sale for legal reasons. There were many, I trust, very many men of good character and proper

---

[1] Herbert Spencer was a leading English political and moral philosopher widely read in the United States during the nineteenth and early twentieth centuries.
[2] That is, the Civil War.

self-respect, who did not push their legal rights to the extent of the law, but there were thousands of two-legged brutes who used the lash on short notice. The prevalence of wife beating has had much to do with the coarse manners and insolent behavior of their own male progeny. As I understand the meaning of law, it is to provide against what an evil doer is apt to do, but our ante-bellum Georgia laws furnished the opportunity to brutal men to exercise their right as masters over wives as well as slaves. What is known as chivalry found no expression on the statute books of Georgia until the Civil War made changes. It exploited itself in courting days, in bowing and scraping in public company, and in personal encounters, which were known as duels. An insult called for a challenge, and then pistols. Nevertheless the law of Georgia allowed any sort of a man to beat his wife, provided the switch was no bigger than his thumb. Glance down at your thumb my dear reader, and then we will proceed a little further.

In the homes where the lash was used the sons either despised the father or concluded it was the proper way to treat women. The daughters, afraid and disgusted, took chances, hoping to do better in selecting kinder masters than their mothers had done.

Those who were fortunate were contented in their ignorance. Those who felt the lash were helpless before the law of the land.

In Georgia before the war, a woman might teach school as a genteel profession — if she was educated. If she was illiterate she could weave or sew, if her rich neighbors gave her such work to do. The school teacher generally married some man with slaves to wait on her. The illiterate woman went to the kitchen and cornfield, like the slave woman of the big plantations. The well-fed negroes made a standing joke on "po-white trash."

Constitutional Convention of 1868

This convention has been abused without mercy, as a radical body, controlled by scalawags and carpet-baggers, but it was the first state convention in Georgia to secure property rights to women who were married. It was said to be a selfish proposition because the vast majority of our men were hopelessly in debt when the war closed. If the woman could claim the property, then there would be a home, a living, and maintenance. Otherwise the dear good man would be in bondage to his obligations. It has proved to be a popular law for the men as well as the women. "Calico pensioners" are still plentiful. And if the man was mean and cruel he could make his wife turn over the proceeds — and if he was suave and polite, he could borrow and forget to pay back. If she was prosperous, he was more so — and he is still amusing himself by putting all things doubtful in *"his wife's name."* And the majority of these "calico pensioners" are almost rabid maniacs in opposition to votes for women!

Votes for Women — Some Objections as Printed in the Papers

It is claimed that women should not vote, because she does not pay her husband's debts, while he is obliged to pay her debts. That is not correct. He can put a little "ad" in the newspapers and nobody will give her credit who sells dry goods or provisions. Others say she shirks jury duty. Georgia women have not had any jury opportunity. Again; she does not perform military duty. I think they are mistaken. The woman provides the material out of which soldiers are made and devotes sixteen years of hard toil towards their raising. Another objects that women can marry men younger than themselves — while men are interdicted in like matters. As the woman is always to be chosen and not the chooser, the objection is invalid. Again, a man cannot say "cuss words" on the street, in presence of women. Ninety-nine times out of a hundred — the foul-mouthed man will say a hundred times worse things in presence of his wife and daughter, and nobody cares to rebuke him. Again, it is urged that women are favored as to hours of labor. These favors have been wrung out of greed and indifference, by the votes of labor organizations, who demanded better treatment to wage-earning girls and married women — because of injured physical conditions. Being poor men with working women they had the votes and said so! It is understood that labor organizations are almost unanimous for Woman Suffrage, because they understand they would themselves be at the mercy of their employers without the ballot. I have seen white women on their all-fours, scrubbing the halls of the great Departments in Washington City, thirty years ago, and nobody protested that these child-bearing women were out of their sphere. In the very shadow of the Capitol dome and in the very offices of the great leaders in political and social economy there is discrimination as to the pay of men and women. Equal work fails to secure equal pay. The thing that is lacking is the vote (compelling attention) and equity (demanded at the ballot box).

Is the Ballot a Right or a Favor?

It is an erroneous idea that has been actively promulgated for a purpose — that women have no claim to the ballot privilege, because they have no title to its possession. One objector says the ballot is a franchise and a dispensation, without any inherent or moral or legal right, as pertaining to women. I claim that they were born into all the rights that are the property of their brothers, born of the same parents and raised in the same home and educated in the same way. The law of inheritance, where parents die intestate, gives to each child, *regardless of sex,* equal shares in the inherited property, and when the property is divided, dollar for dollar, the daughters own their parts as legally as the sons own their parts, but the law of the land gives to the males liberty to say how and when and by whom, that property shall be taxed, and denies to the females this essential and inherent right. The right to own property is allowed to every person in a republican form of government, regardless of sex, but the right to say how, or when, or by whom that property is to be taxed is denied to one half the citizens of the United States, except in the States which have been enfranchised by the good sense and common honesty of the men of those States — after due consideration, and with the chivalric instinct that differentiates the coarse brutal male from the gentlemen of our nation. Shall the men of the South be less generous, less chivalrous? They have given the Southern women more praise than the man of the West — but judged by their actions Southern men have been less sincere. Honeyed phrases are pleasant to listen to, but the sensible women of our country would prefer more substantial gifts. . . .

It is said that women are represented by their husbands at the ballot box. This is not true; of the ten millions of unmarried women who have nobody to vote for them, there are between eight and nine millions of unmarried men, who vote for nobody but themselves. *And nobody votes for the drunkard's wife?* There are as many widows in this country as widowers. As a rule they manage well their business affairs and they were forced to learn under difficulties. They deserve the ballot because their property is taxed to the limit and beyond, and they are not allowed to protest. *Women make fine teachers.* A callow youth can vote at 21, while his capable teacher *if a woman,* is forbidden to vote. Women are the mainstays in public schools. They are not only forbidden the vote, but their pay is reduced because of their sex. They make superior stenographers, but while their pay may reach fifty dollars a month the young man in trousers gets from seventy-five to a hundred, with no better work — and according to common report, not so reliable as to fidelity and regular habits. The more I think about these inequalities and this manifest injustice, the more I am tempted to eulogize the heathens who lived on the Ganges river, and who drowned the girl babies, because they were unfit to live! . . .

Some years ago, in 1901, I was invited by the Legislature to address the members of House and Senate in joint session on the "Infirmities of our Public School System." I was placed on the Speaker's rostrum, with Governor Allen Candler on my left and Speaker Howell on my right. The hall was packed — floor and gallery. Crowds stood because there were no vacant seats. After I came home Governor Candler wrote me a long and approving letter. As it bears directly on the present subject, I will copy a few lines at this time. "The truth is, Mrs. Felton, we started wrong in 1865. We had been overpowered by our Northern invaders. The flower of our manhood had perished in battle. Those of our men population who had survived the conflict and returned to their ruined homes were disarmed and put on parole. The fanatics whom the fortunes of war had enthroned in Washington first demanded that we repudiate our war debt. *We did it.* Secondly we were ordered to emancipate our slaves, and *we did it.* Thirdly they demanded that we arm them with the ballot to protect them in their newly acquired freedom, *and we did it.* Then they said we must educate them to make good citizens out of them and for thirty years we have been taxing ourselves almost to the verge of confiscation to fit them for citizenship and we have failed. Education has no more effect on them morally and intellectually than it has physically. God made them negroes and we cannot make them white folks by education. We are on the wrong track. We must turn back. *We must limit suffrage to virtue and intelligence. The tax payers are in the minority and in almost every county there is an unreliable and irresponsible vote which constitutes the balance of power and the law makers consult this class, rather than the interest of those who sit on juries — who pay the taxes — fight the battles and bear the burthens of Government."* In this connection I will inquire where can you find this: virtue and intelligence unless your wives, mothers, sisters, and daughters come to your relief?

If Women Do Not Want to Vote — No Objection

It is a stock argument with our anti-suffrage friends that women do not care to vote, will not vote, etc., etc. This can only be proven when the test is applied. There are those who say they have all the rights they want — have never needed better laws than we have had in Georgia since it was a colony, etc. Such arguments were presented to the Legislature last summer by highly educated Georgia ladies. To these

I can only say if they prefer to hug their chains, I have no sort of objection. If they accept the position of *inferiority,* why try to impress them with repeated arguments against serfdom in mind, body or estate? If they choose to be *parasites,* of course they can be such. If they can afford to lower their own claims below idiots, the insane and the criminal classes and are content to allow negro men superior voting privileges to themselves *why disturb their stagnant equilibrium?* I make no appeal to that class of our women. At that very time when these distinguished Georgia women were assuring our legislators that Georgia women had all they needed — all they were entitled to, and more, there were anxious Georgia women who were pleading for a more humane age of consent, as Georgia has adopted ten years — lower than any other state or territory or dependency, except Hawaii, on this continent. A little ten year old child is considered sufficiently able to protect her virtue from the wiles of the libertine and the debasing lures of a procuress! Time and time again have these faithful women appealed to a stubborn Legislature to alter those figures, to no effect. At that very time we were imploring the Legislature to allow qualified women to practice law in Georgia, without effect. At that very time, patriotic women were appealing for a law to keep small children away from cotton factories where their no-account daddies were using the money they earned: in soft drinks, cigarettes, and other indulgences and doing nothing for themselves. At that very time these patriotic women were pleading for equal pay for equal work — for women. At that very time, they were asking that bigamists should receive their just deserts. At that very time, they were pleading for a law to give the woman *equal partnership with her husband in her own children.* At that very time women were giving time, strength, and constant attendance, hoping that our legislators would devise ways and means to perfect our State-wide prohibition law. At that very time Atlanta was in a perfect turmoil and the "Men and Religion" movement were thundering in the daily papers about vice conditions in the shadow of the dome of the Capitol of Georgia! (Of all the helpless things under the shining sun in the Commonwealth of Georgia, it is a poor, unfortunate girl, without money and without work — when her seducer walks the streets with head up and no hindrance!) And to no effect!

Nero fiddled while Rome was burning! —

Satisfied with high positions in women's organizations, to which they had themselves been chosen, *by the votes* of their own colleagues, they were manifestly ignorant of what was going on, looking to the relief of their own sex in matters that actually took hold on life and death. It is needless to say that many patriotic efforts were repelled by such lack of sympathy and non-appreciation of patriotic women who were pleading for relief under difficulties — in behalf of those women who were poor and unfortunate and helpless. It was to be expected that common, coarse men should vote "no." They had been doubtless raised when the rule of the rod no bigger than a man's thumb prevailed, and breeding will tell, in humans as well as in cattle!

The Serious Mistake

When we consider how many men have become tyrants and oppressors because of the brute idea that women were only made for man's use, and abuse, the breadth and depth of human misery that has been going on and is daily caused by this one mistake in our dealings with the sexes, is most appalling. Marriage between a master and a slave was obliged to be debasing to both. Marriage in its true meaning rests upon absolute equality between the sexes as to rights and privileges — legal, political, and social. Marriage has an exalted meaning for those who have clear vision on this line. The hope for the regeneration of mankind is dependent upon a community of interest in all things material, as well as affection in matrimony. Marriage is a partnership, and the children are blessed, when the father accords to the mother every right that he claims for himself, with honest dealing and mutual respect from both partners. The family in its best form is a school for mutual tenderness, mutual sympathy, self-sacrifice, forgetfulness of self, and four-square dealing as to benefits and obligations. Honorable marriage is the only conservator of National health and of National prosperity!

Years ago Dr. Powell, then at the head of the State Sanitarium, told me that seventy-five per cent of the insane women came from the poor farms in Georgia. Like dumb-driven cattle, the brain broke down. The treadmill of all hard work and no recreation wore out body and soul! The delicately pampered females in modern Paris and New York dwindle to decay as did they of old Rome. The poor, illiterate woman and the idle parasite woman amount to less than nothing. One is crushed with her burden, and the other is only a butterfly of fashion. One great defect in both cases lies in the lack of co-operation in their homes. They have had no preparation for life and its realities. Of course these women have had no experience in governmental affairs — would be ciphers everywhere. But they are not alone. There are tens of thousands of men in this country who know as little, after having the ballot privilege since they were twenty-one years of age. The mire of politics has been too much for them. As Governor Candler truly said, they are totally unreliable and irresponsible. Why should such men dictate laws to educated, high-toned and capable women?

A Word to Men Concerning Their Mothers

Whatever you may have lacked in life, you surely have had a mother. The great majority of men are willing to accord decent respect to these authors of their being — but there is also a large class which has no respect for any woman. It is well to remind those who sneer and jeer, that every mother's son of them owes his social status to his mother. It is the rule in royal houses of Europe. A morganatic wife could not give heirs to the great kingdoms or empires of modern Europe today. The mother must have the blood of kings and emperors in her own veins to mother the crown princes of the old world. In the time of slavery in the United States, slave mothers always made slave children. A white father did not give freedom to the slave woman's child — but the degenerate white woman who sunk herself below the pity of her sex, and outlawed herself beyond recovery, she gave them freedom, no matter how dark complexioned. It was the law before the war — they obtained freedom through the blood of the white mother. On the other hand the degenerate white man was willing to put his offspring in the kitchen and corn field, and speculators bought and sold them on the block, the overseer's lash drove them while the stars were shining before day, and while the stars were shining after dark, and the law of the land said "slaves," because the mother was a slave. Some few slaves were emancipated by their owners, for various reasons, but the free-born, Afro-American came to his freedom by the white blood of his mother.

Freedom belongs to the white woman as her inherent right. Whatever belongs to the freedom of these United States belongs to the white woman. Her Anglo-Saxon forefathers, fleeing from English tyranny won this country from savage tribes and again from English bayonets, by the expenditure of blood and treasure. Whatever was won by these noble men of the Revolution was inherited alike by sons and daughters. Fifty years from now this country will hold up hands in holy horror that deadly intoxicants were ever sold to debauch men and women, and also that any man or set of men in America should assume to themselves the authority to deny to free-born white women of America the ballot, which is the badge and synonym of freedom!

Lame Excuses

We are told that women will vote as men do — vote their prejudices and go off half-cocked in election matters. The first thing the women of California did was to vote out saloons as election booths and put the ballot boxes in clean school houses. One was owned by the liquor traffic and the other by the State. And we are told that white women might vote, but what about negro cooks? As our men in Georgia have paddled down the voting stream for nearly a half century, with negro men cooks and barbers, etc., we will not cross that bridge before we come to it. They tell us that the women of the underworld would crowd the polls. The authorities will tell you that every voter must register in their own names, with place of residence, and this they never do, if it can be helped. A few women like Mrs. Russell Sage, Mrs. Harriman, and Mrs. Hetty Green own one-third of the wealth of this country. Their chauffeurs and negro butlers can vote, while they are denied the ballot.

You have known some men who never could have reached Congress except through bad men's votes. Lorimer, the Republican, went to the Senate by bribing Democratic legislators in Illinois. Roberts, of Indiana, has gone to the State prison, after being a Democratic candidate for Governor, because he bought and sold votes in Indianapolis. Women could not possibly do worse than that! Statistics tell us that there are thirty men criminals to one woman criminal, and there are as many women as men in this country. It is said that women are keen after the offices. I am not posted on that part of it, but the very idea of opposition to the chronic office seeker will send cold chills down his spine and make his teeth chatter.

I have heard stalwart men complaining that women stenographers were robbing men of their own employment. I thought there was still plenty of out-doors for the complainant, where he could improve his muscle as well as his temper. If women must stay in the home, the man should exercise abroad. I would like to print a list of great Queens, like Victoria and Tsi Ann of China, of great astronomers, great singers, great novelists, great teachers, great leaders in philanthropy like Frances Willard — all women; but my space forbids. I will mention modest Queen Wilhemina of Holland, who sits steady in the boat while Kings and Emperors are fairly bursting with blood-thirsty rage against their opponents. She is the only woman ruler in Europe, and apparently has more self-control than any of them under most embarrassing conditions. If women can make good queens, they might be tolerated as plain voters in a republic.

New Men as Well as New Women

The "New Woman" is often criticised. The term is never applied as a compliment, but there also is the "New Man" to be reckoned with. This New Man has given the ballot privilege in extenso to between five and six millions of voting women. They are giving a partial ballot in a dozen other States. These States are fast coming into full enfranchisement. Today, in a presidential primary, these voting women will hold the balance of power. And we, who claim the vote as our right; inherent — moral and legal right, are as proud to be the daughters of our fathers, as the daughters of our mothers. We belong to a womanhood like our mothers did, which was never bought and sold for a European title, or made a millionaire's plaything to be treated like a pet cat — fed on cream and purr in idleness. We come of a race who shirked no dangers, nor cowered in fear. These women of our blood stood side by side with their mates when it was considered treason to the King to sign the oath of Allegiance to Independance in 1776–'78. It can never be dishonorable to unfurl the banner of freedom in a free country, but it will be the New Man who will give the ballot to his mother, his wife, his sister, and his daughter. He has had clear vision in the great West. The Star of Empire is turned, and leading to the East. He knows that the elevation of women has given vitality and strength to mankind. He knows that the standard of mothers is the final standard of all races of men. He knows as the mother's brain weakens, the brain of her son weakens; as her muscles soften, his child's muscles soften; as she decays, the people decay in every station in life. The parasitism of child-bearing women has always weakened the race. The mother of his children must be given the best, that she may do her best. While he knows there are women who are more selfish than patriotic, more indifferent to the duty of child-bearing than to society fribbles, and there are those who prefer like Helen of Troy to be passed along from man to man, and who will, like Cleopatra, entice great men to their overthrow; yet he also knows that the coming mothers of the United States must be prepared to understand the principles of government, to meet the exigencies that doubtful conditions are forcing upon the country. He knows that he can trust the wife of his bosom with the nearest and dearest interests of his existence. The call of the age is for wise and capable women, and the New Man understands that his mate must be his comrade and likewise his friend in every emergency.

This woman's movement is a great movement of the sexes toward each other, with common ideals as to government, as well as common ideals in domestic life, where fully developed manhood must seek and find its real mate in the mother of his children, as well as the solace of his home. The time has long past since the hard-drinking, fox-hunting, high-playing country squire was excused because of his generosity and hospitality. He was not the equal of his sober mate, whose hand held the distaff, who made good cheer from kitchen to drawing-room. The call of the age is for partnership in the family, in the church, in the State and National affairs, between men and women.

The brothel, the gaming table, the race course, and habits of physical excess are still with us, but the hope of this Nation lies in the broad-minded men who gladly acclaim woman's success in every field of literature, science, music, art, in the organized professions, and great national philanthropies. These are the men to whom we look for the early recognition of women everywhere, in the everyday duties, with everyday experience, and mutual acquaintance with the various problems of government.

Selected Bibliography

GENERAL STUDIES

Ayers, Edward L. *The Promise of the New South: Life after Reconstruction.* New York: Oxford University Press, 1992.
Clayton, Bruce L. *The Savage Ideal: Intolerance and Intellectual Leadership in the South, 1890–1914.* Baltimore: Johns Hopkins University Press, 1972.
Grantham, Dewey W., Jr. *Southern Progressivism: The Reconciliation of Progress and Tradition.* Knoxville: University of Tennessee Press, 1983.
Link, William A. *The Paradox of Southern Progressivism, 1880–1930.* Chapel Hill: University of North Carolina Press, 1992.
Rabinowitz, Howard. *The First New South, 1865–1920.* Arlington Heights, Ill: Harlan Davidson, 1992.
Woodward, C. Vann. *Origins of the New South, 1877–1913.* Baton Rouge: Louisiana State University Press, 1951.

RACE

Gilmore, Glenda. "Gender and Jim Crow: Women and the Politics of White Supremacy in North Carolina, 1896–1920." Ph.D. diss., University of North Carolina at Chapel Hill, 1992.
Hall, Jacquelyn Dowd. *Revolt against Chivalry: Jessie Daniel Ames and the Women's Campaign against Lynching.* New York: Columbia University Press, 1979.
Harlan, Louis R. *Booker T. Washington.* 2 vols. New York: Oxford University Press, 1972–83.
Kirby, Jack Temple. *Darkness at the Dawning: Race and Reform in the Progressive South.* Philadelphia: J. B. Lippincott, 1972.
Rouse, Jacqueline Anne. *Lugenia Burns Hope: Black Southern Reformer.* Athens: University of Georgia Press, 1989.

PROHIBITION

Clark, Norman. *Deliver Us from Evil: An Interpretation of American Prohibition.* New York: Norton, 1976.
Kerr, K. Austin. *Organized for Prohibition: A New History of the Anti-Saloon League.* New Haven: Yale University Press, 1985.

Pearson, Charles Chilton, and J. Edwin Hendricks. *Liquor and Anti-Liquor in Virginia, 1619–1919*. Durham, N.C.: Duke University Press, 1967.

Sellers, James Benson. *The Prohibition Movement in Alabama, 1702 to 1943*. Chapel Hill: University of North Carolina Press, 1943.

Whitener, Daniel Jay. *Prohibition in North Carolina, 1715–1945*. Chapel Hill: University of North Carolina Press, 1946.

CHILD LABOR

Carlton, David L. *Mill and Town in South Carolina, 1880–1920*. Baton Rouge: Louisiana State University Press, 1982.

Davidson, Elizabeth Huey. *Child Labor Legislation in the Southern Textile States*. Chapel Hill: University of North Carolina Press, 1939.

Hall, Jacquelyn, James Leloudis, Robert Korstad, Mary Murphy, and Christopher B. Daly. *Like a Family: The Making of a Southern Cotton Mill World*. Chapel Hill: University of North Carolina Press, 1987.

Trattner, Walter I. *Crusade for the Children: A History of the National Child Labor Committee and Child Labor Reform in America*. Chicago: Quadrangle Books, 1970.

BLACK EDUCATION

Anderson, James D. *The Education of Blacks in the South, 1860–1935*. Chapel Hill: University of North Carolina Press, 1988.

Hanchett, Thomas W. "The Rosenwald Schools and Black Education in North Carolina." *North Carolina Historical Review* 65 (Oct. 1988): 387–427.

Harlan, Louis R. *Separate and Unequal: Public School Campaigns and Racism in the Southern Seaboard States, 1901–1915*. Chapel Hill: University of North Carolina Press, 1958.

Kousser, J. Morgan. "Progressivism — For Middle-Class Whites Only: North Carolina Education, 1880–1910." *Journal of Southern History* 46 (May 1980): 169–84.

Link, William A. *A Hard Country and a Lonely Place: Schooling, Society, and Reform in Rural Virginia, 1870–1920*. Chapel Hill: University of North Carolina Press, 1986.

Margo, Robert A. *Race and Schooling in the South, 1880–1930: An Economic History*. Chicago: University of Chicago Press, 1990.

NEW WOMEN

Green, Elna C. "Those Opposed: The Antisuffragists of North Carolina, 1900–1920." *North Carolina Historical Review* 67 (July 1990): 315–33.

Johnson, Kenneth R. "The Woman Suffrage Movement in Florida." Ph.D. diss., Florida State University, 1966.

Scott, Anne Firor. *The Southern Lady from Pedestal to Politics, 1880–1930*. Chicago: University of Chicago Press, 1970.

Taylor, Antoinette Elizabeth. *The Woman Suffrage Movement in Tennessee*. New York: Bookman Associates, 1957.

Wheeler, Marjorie Spruill. *New Women of the New South: The Leaders of the Woman Suffrage Movement in the Southern States.* New York: Oxford University Press, 1993.

Index